# Homemade Christmas

*Holiday recipes, gifts, decorations and memories to treasure*

A Portion of the Proceeds of This Book
Benefits the Marine Toys for Tots Foundation.

MARINE
TOYS FOR TOTS
FOUNDATION

*Anne Darrah*
Artist / Book Designer

*Mary Harvey Gurley*
Writer

## TRADERY
### H·O·U·S·E

Library of Congress Card Catalog Number:
95-61098
ISBN: 1-879958-27-9

For additional copies,
use the order form in the back of the book, or call
The Wimmer Companies, Inc., 1-800-727-1034.

Printed in the USA by

WIMMER
The Wimmer Companies, Inc.
Memphis • Dallas

# Traditions Abound

BY MARY HARVEY GURLEY

As people from every nation have come to call this country home, they have brought with them their holiday traditions. In the Southwest, there are Spanish and Mexican traditions woven into their holiday celebrations, including the feast of the Lady of Guadeloupe. Swedish Americans celebrate St. Lucia's Day. German descendants proudly claim the introduction of the Christmas tree to the New World's holiday tradition. American Jews keep Chanukah or Hanukkah, the Jewish Festival of Lights. African Americans enjoy the winter festival of Kwanzaa.

Every person who immigrated to the United States added something to the tradition and fabric of our American Christmas. Nowhere else in the world could such a fun diversity of traditions exist. *Homemade Christmas* gathers the ideas and spirit of an American holiday season that celebrates not only the heritage of the region we call home but also the cultures of our former homelands.

Though our celebrations and religious beliefs may be different, the thread that keeps them consistent is their focus on festive foods, good friends, and the fellowship of family. New customs and traditions continue to develop even today. As a young couple begins a home and starts a family, they blend the traditions of two households, add new ideas, and pass those along to their children. If we traveled from city to town, we would find thousands of holiday customs, old and new. Almost every household would tell of a tradition they cherished that would be different from their neighbor's or even another member of their family.

# A Special Season

Christmas is a time when our hearts and minds ache for tradition, family, and the warmth of home. Aromas from the kitchen conjure up thoughts of childhood fantasies. Taking a cold winter afternoon to make a plate of Fantasy Fudge or Christmas cookies with your children will create a lifetime of memories for them.

Colonial Williamsburg, the site of one of the earliest American celebrations, used evergreens, boxwoods, and citrus fruit to welcome in the holidays, as they do today. And one of the most lasting symbols of that era, the pineapple, still signals visitors that they will find a warm welcome within—usually to dine on ham or duck.

A Southwest holiday likely includes a piñata as the focus of the celebration, and a cowboy Christmas tree. The bill of fare might highlight spicy foods and cool drinks. The South, so steeped in tradition, decorates with their native magnolias, and the menu would not be complete without a sweet potato casserole and holiday ham.

Italian Americans would not consider setting the holiday table without plates of pasta and lasagna to accompany their turkey. All these illustrate that the traditions of our ancestral homelands have woven their way into the creation of a beautiful holiday tapestry.

Today, family may mean more than one household. Americans, young and old, are searching for traditions to bring their families closer together and ensure that their children have a heritage to call their own.

In the immigrant days of America, new citizens dropped the traditions of their homelands, eager for "Americanization." However, it is not unusual in many homes today, for the parents to research the holiday celebrations of their ancestral homelands and include them in their own. People want to feel a continuity of tradition, and know they have passed on to their children a piece of history and culture.

# Welcome to the Holidays

*I*f you feel your holiday celebrations have become hollow, void of meaning and tradition, *Homemade Christmas* offers ideas and projects in which the entire family can take part. The recipes and food ideas are practical, and we promise not to chain you to the kitchen for days.

Don't allow yourself to be overwhelmed with the "busy-ness" of the season. Chart another plan of action this holiday season. The long Thanksgiving weekend provides a good time to begin decorating the outside of your home. The weekend after Thanksgiving, you might consider decorating the interior of your home. There are numerous decorating ideas included in *Homemade Christmas* that can be accomplished with just a little time—and just a little money.

The following weekend, plan a light supper and trim the tree with family and friends. Preparing over a few weekends allows you to enjoy each step.

Schedule cooking and assembling holiday gifts in the evenings. You will find fun ideas for gifts, many from the kitchen—including a Boursin cheese, cookie and candy recipes.

If the holiday season wouldn't be the same without a party, try something new. Our Dickens Christmas party helps you celebrate the holidays just like they did in Merry Olde England. And don't forget the kids; our Reindeer Party will long be remembered by the little elves.

A Homemade Christmas—or Thanksgiving, Hanukkah, or Kwanzaa—is just a stop away. Find a spirited holiday beverage and a simple appetizer, put your feet up, and wander through these pages to create the holiday season of your dreams.

Happy Holidays!

# What's Waiting Inside . . .

## Enchanting Holiday Decorations

Something magical occurs during the holiday season, as the lights of the tree and wreath illuminate our homes. We seem to concentrate on making our homes enchanted winter wonderlands filled with memory-making magic. The decorating and homemaking traditions in this chapter echo our wishes to re-create the spirits of the season and to help you find new ways to add holiday magic to your home and hearth.

*Pages 9 to 26*

## Memories, Tastes, and Spirits

There is no other aspect of the holiday season that creates more anxiety than selecting the right gifts for friends and family. If your budget is tight and the list is long, review the ideas in this chapter—gifts from the heart and the kitchen. Gift giving is an art, and its practice need not break your bank account or drain your energy. Giving of yourself is one of the greatest holiday gifts.

*Pages 27 to 52*

## Setting the Stage

### Menus and Entertaining

Holiday entertaining is much like a theater production. You are the director. Your guests are the stars. Your home, the food, and decorations set the stage. Included in this chapter are menus from folks around the country and the memories associated with their menu suggestions. Seven great party ideas follow the regional menus—with ideas and recipes to weave into your holiday entertaining.

**Pages 53 to 72**

---

## Recipes for Festive Food

### From New England Traditional to California Casual

The holiday season is the time that everyone feels compelled to pull out all the stops. We expect our meals to be magical, delicious—and simple. We want to try new festive foods for our families and friends, and we want to be certain the new recipes won't flop. The recipes in this chapter are festive and the beverages spirited. Now all you have to do is make the company memorable. **Pages 73 to 146**

---

## Sugar and Spice

Think back to holiday memories of childhood. What comes to mind? Baking cookies or fudge? Preparing an elegant dessert for a holiday dinner? It's the season of sweet memories— including chocolate ones. In this chapter find an array of memorable sugar and spice delights for your family to snack on around the tree, to bring to the office, to offer for a friend's holiday party, and to exchange with friends, both near and far. **Pages 147 to 214**

### And Chocolate Delight

## Keeping Notes
**Pages 215 to 216**

## Index
**Pages 217 to 222**

# Special Thanks To...

🌀 *Anne Darrah,* of New Iberia, Louisiana, for her creative talents in producing the delightful cover design, book design, calligraphy, and wonderful illustrations flowing throughout these pages.

🌀 *Ed Bamberger,* of Flower Mound, Texas, for his editing expertise.

🌀 *Mary Harvey Gurley,* of Memphis, Tennessee, for her well-chosen, memory-producing words for the introductions, decorating and gift chapters, and party themes, as well as the many delicious recipes she shared for the book.

🌀 *Ann Hultz, Peggy Larkin,* and *Julie Wilson,* of Memphis, for their inspiring holiday decorating ideas.

🌀 To those folks around the country who shared their special menus, recipes, and holiday thoughts—*Candy Coe Richardson, Peter D. Franklin, Women's League of Adat Ari El Synagogue, Linda Merritt Allen, Lucille Hooker, Timothy Malm, Barbara Andrews, Mary Gunderson, Susan Grohman,* and *Marcelle Bienvenu.*

🌀 And to all the others whose short stories of holidays and traditions bring fond remembrances to all of us.

# A Winter Wonderland

*Enchanting Holiday Decorations*

*S*omething magical occurs during the holiday season, as the lights of the tree and wreath illuminate our homes. We seem to forget the worn furniture and empty corners and concentrate on making our homes enchanted winter wonderlands filled with memory-making magic.

From the wreath at the door to the Christmas tree, our holiday decorations signal that the festival season has begun. Our neighbor who hangs the first Christmas light ignites our competitive nature. We hurry to bring out our holiday decor to ensure that everyone knows our homes and hearts are celebrating the season.

Harvest and Thanksgiving provide us the opportunity to decorate with wheat, straw, and pumpkins. A harvest scene at the front door in late October ushers in the season—and the harvest look gives way to red, green, silver, and gold in early December.

In Jewish households the menorah signals the season of light, as the Advent wreath does in Christian homes. Our decorations are symbolic of our unique heritage and religious beliefs.

Homemade Christmas offers a multitude of new holiday decorations to blend with regional favorites and your family's long-standing holiday traditions. Consider making a topiary for your Christmas celebration and gift giving. A Kissing Ball can take the place of a sprig of mistletoe and a Cowboy Christmas tree is a whimsical reminder of the Southwest's great history.

The smells of Christmas are as much of the decor as the tree, wreaths, and manger scenes. The aroma of evergreens, potpourri, and fresh-baked delights fill our minds with Christmas memories.

# Tiered Wreath Tree

*A*lmost like a Christmas merry-go-round, this tiered wreath tree offers a unique decoration steeped in holiday style. If you have a corner dining table or another place you would like a Christmas tree, use this wreath tree rather than a miniature evergreen. If you have access to herbs, such as rosemary and thyme, using them to style this wreath will add a pleasant aroma to the entire room. Fresh evergreens used in place of herbs may be more accessible and just as aromatic. If you like to use a decoration for several years, then try silk roping or three silk wreaths to fashion this charming centerpiece. As wreaths are always a decorating favorite, this unique design will draw plenty of compliments from friends and family.

- Mix the plaster of paris in a bucket. Place the dowel into a small plastic pot, tape over hole (if there is one), and pour 2 to 3 inches of plaster into the pot. Make sure the dowel is straight. Allow plaster to dry.

- Make three circles of wire: 5½ inches, 7½ inches, and 9½ inches. (You can find grapevine wreaths in various sizes if you prefer that look to the plain wire.) Overlap the wire ends. Wrap each piece of wire with the green floral tape.

- Divide plant material so that you have similar kinds for each tier. Wrap small bunches of your evergreen or plant material with spool wire and secure to the frame or wreath. Continue until all three tiers are covered.

- Wrap ribbon around the dowel, and glue it to both ends. Cut the cording into two (40-inch) lengths. Hold the pieces together, and knot one end. Tack the knot to the top of the dowel to make four equal streamers.

*(Continued on page 12)*

## Materials

Plaster of Paris
½-inch dowel
(18 inches long)
Container
(a flower pot)
Small plastic pot
Clothesline wire
Wire cutters
Green floral tape
Spool of floral wire
Ribbon and cording
Glue
Tacks
Decorative container
(basket or pot)
Gravel
Greenery

❧ Place the plastic pot into the decorative pot. Fill with gravel to stabilize.

❧ Place the largest wreath over the dowel, then the middle, and then the smallest. Tie the smallest wreath evenly with the four pieces of cording. Ensure that it hangs evenly and is parallel with the table surface. Repeat with the other two wreaths. Add decorative ornaments for accents.

# Kissing Ball

*Found most often in Williamsburg as a traditional decoration, a kissing ball hangs from chandeliers or doorways as an alternative to the traditional sprig of mistletoe. Use fresh greenery, or make it with artificial greens to hang year after year.*

## Materials

½ block floral foam
Chicken wire or garden netting
Twine
#18 floral wire
Clippers
Evergreen, boxwood
Ribbon

❧ Soak the foam (unless you are making an artificial one).

❧ Wrap ½ block of the floral foam with chicken wire or netting. Secure with floral wire.

❧ Insert a 10-inch piece of floral wire through the center of the floral foam, and make a hook shape at the bottom.

❧ Pull the wire up from the top until it is embedded in the foam.

❧ Make a loop in the wire at the top, and use this to attach ribbons or another hanger. Insert the boxwood, evergreen, or mistletoe stems into the foam, filling the whole area with plant material.

❧ Attach ribbons and bows to the top and bottom.

*Homemade Christmas*

# Cowboy Christmas Tree

Try a taste of the Southwest to have a root tootin' Christmas. Begin with a sparse evergreen tree. First place chile pepper or cactus lights on the tree instead of regular colored lights. Roping, tied like a cowboy lasso, can adorn the tree like garland, or tie bandanna handkerchiefs together for the same effect. The handkerchiefs can also be tied into bows, fans, or ribbons to scatter around the tree.

Typical ornaments for this type tree might include cow, cactus, boot, and hat ornaments and cowboy boot cookies. Sheriff badges can hang on the tree or be party favors. And top it all off with a cowboy hat.

# Piñata

*Breaking a piñata is the highlight of Mexican festivities during the holidays. A piñata is a large, hanging papier-mâché ornament filled with candies and gifts that hangs from above. You can buy piñatas at party stores and gift shops, or you can make your own.*

- To make the paste, put 1 cup of flour in a bowl, and slowly add water. Mix until the consistency of thin pancake batter.

- Blow up the balloon, tie it, and rub the surface with a thin coat of Vaseline.

- Place the balloon in the flower pot, and tie down by attaching a string to the balloon end. Run it through the hole in the bottom of the pot, and set the string under the pot.

- Dip newspaper strips into the flour paste, wet them completely, and apply to the balloon. Cover the balloon with one layer of newspaper, overlapping the pieces. Smooth each piece after placing it on the balloon. Do not cover the area of the balloon in the flower pot.

*(Continued on page 14)*

- Apply two more coats of newspaper over the entire balloon.

- Allow the papier-mâché to dry completely—up to 24 hours.

- Pop the balloon, remove it, and remove any leftover Vaseline; let dry another 24 hours.

- Paint the piñata with two coats of acrylic paint. Decorate with tissue paper.

- Puncture four holes around the rim of the piñata by pushing a nail through. Put strings through the holes.

- Fill the piñata with candy and presents, and hang at a comfortable height from the ceiling. Blindfold each child. Turn the child around three times and give three chances to break the piñata with a long stick.

# Potpourri Envelopes

*For a lovely fragrant holiday remembrance, create these potpourri envelopes. Include them in Christmas cards, use as hostess gifts, or place them as favors at each setting of the table.*

## Materials

2- to 3-inch-wide, wire-edged ribbon (gauzy gold, red, or green)
Hot glue gun
Potpourri
Holiday cording

- Cut a 10-inch strand of ribbon. Fold up 4 inches of ribbon.

- Glue gun each side of the 4 inches, affixing 4 inches against 4 inches and leaving a 2-inch ribbon opening.

- After glue has dried, fill with potpourri.

- Fold the 2 inches of ribbon down and glue to seal the envelope.

- Attach cording, a name card for place settings, or place, as is, in holiday cards.

# Thanksgiving Centerpieces

For a traditional Thanksgiving touch to your table, use the small plentiful pumpkins of October and November. Dig out a small portion of the top of the pumpkin, and glue fresh flowers in the top. You can also use greenery or any sort of dried flowers with berries. Fresh flowers give the table a warm attractive feeling, even if the weather has turned cold. If the pumpkins are small enough, you can place them at individual place settings. Or you can cluster three to five of them for your main centerpiece.

# Peppermint Wreath

Children love to help make wreaths to feel part of the holiday decorating process. Using either a grapevine wreath or a straw wreath as a base, attach real peppermint candy canes around it using a hot glue gun (adults should perform this function, not children). Place greenery, green roping, or green ribbon between the canes; glue them in place. Finish it off with a bow in the center or tied to the wreath. Besides being a decoration, peppermint wreaths double as great gifts — especially for teachers.

# Chair Corsage

To create a dramatic effect in your dining room, make chair corsages to match your centerpiece. You can make them for all your chairs or just for the guest of honor's chair. After selecting the flowers to make your centerpiece, buy extra for your corsages. Gather 4 to 5 flowers, and twist the stems with floral wire. Using ribbon that matches your dining room or centerpiece, make a bow (see page 21). Once the bow is finished, place the flowers at the center of the bow. Tie the wire from the flowers to the leftover bow wire. Tie the wire or streamers to your chair. For the holiday season, try gold ribbon and white carnations with baby's breath for a stunning look or festive plaid ribbons with holly and greenery. Remember this idea for showers and parties throughout the year; some hostesses do this with silk flowers for a year-round decoration.

# Decorating Your Stairwell

Fresh green roping looks and smells wonderful when gracing a stairwell during the holidays; however, if you use the artificial roping, you will have it from year to year. Attach the green roping to the banister at the top of the stairs; then swag it down and through your banister. Using pine and evergreen roping is an attractive combination. So the swags stay in place, tie them with heavy nylon cord or florist wire. Swag a colored ribbon around and through the greenery. Use the same ribbon to add large bows at the beginning and end of the banister. Line your stairs with poinsettias and small baskets filled with pine cones and Christmas ornaments.

## Kumquat Centerpiece

This centerpiece will receive "oohs" and "aahs" from your holiday guests. You don't have to tell them how simple it is.

Purchase two glass chimneys for the side pieces, and place a grapevine tree or a small artificial Christmas tree as the focus between the chimneys. If you need to make the grapevine tree, form the shape by circling the grapevine around and around, getting smaller until it peaks at the top. Then cut off the leftover vine. Hot glue the pieces up and around the tree until it's secure. If you use a small artificial tree, it is already made in the shape you need. Decorate your tree with Christmas ornaments, small dried flowers, or berries to color coordinate with the kumquats and pomegranates that will be used in the chimneys.

Fill the glass chimneys with kumquats and pomegranates. Sprinkle evergreen potpourri from the top of this glass containers. It will fall in different places around the kumquats, so the green against

the orange/coral is very pretty. You will need to replenish the fruits, depending on how long ahead you decorate; however, this decoration could be used throughout the winter season.

Place a table runner underneath the arrangement, coordinating your colors with the kumquats and pomegranates.

# Moss Topiary

*oday toparies are very much in vogue for florists and decorators. But they are nothing new—the design has been a fashionable gardening and decorating idea for centuries. The people of Colonial Williamsburg often used a topiary of evergreen and dried flowers to brighten winter decor as well as provide a pleasant aroma for their rooms. Though moss is the simplest material to work with, try adding dried flowers, golden sprayed nuts and pods, or potpourri as your skill increases. Topiaries serve as wonderful decorations and much-appreciated gifts.*

## Materials

**Plastic flower pot**
**Gold spray paint**
**Plaster of paris**
**Topiary trunk, tree limb, or dowel rod**
**Styrofoam ball**
**Hot glue gun and glue sticks**
**Moss**
**Sphagnum moss**

Cover plastic flower pot holes with aluminum foil or heavy paper.

Paint pot with gold spray paint.

Mix plaster with water, following directions on the bag. Fill plastic pot two-thirds full with plaster mix. Position stick for tree trunk upright in the plaster. Let dry overnight.

Using knife, cut hole in styrofoam ball for trunk. Spread out sheets of moss and glue to styrofoam ball until it is covered. You can overlap moss. Glue dried flowers, berries, etc., onto the moss, as desired.

Attach ball to trunk with hot glue. Cover plaster in base with sphagnum moss.

*Homemade Christmas*

You can complete this same ideas by finding an attractive branch and securing it in the plaster of paris. After it dries, cover the base with sphagnum moss, and decorate the tree with seasonal ornaments. Place it on a mirror so the ornaments sparkle. (This tree can be used for all holidays decorated in various themes.)

# Mantel Swag

*For centuries, people have adorned their mantels with fresh greenery and dried materials in a swag arrangement. There are many types of swags; this one includes dried materials interspersed with greenery. For the simplest swag, start with evergreen strands already wired together from the Christmas tree vendors in your area and just wire additional material to the existing base.*

## Materials

Clothesline
Wire cutters
3 nails with heads
Hammer
Pliers
20-gauge floral wire
Brown or green floral tape
Sprigs of pine or other evergreen
Pine cones
Dried hydrangea or other dried flowers
Dried seed pods
Bows

- Measure your mantel, and cut two pieces of clothesline that are half the length plus 10 inches to allow for the dip of the swags.

- Drive nails slanting upward at each corner of the mantel and in the middle.

- Make wire loops at the ends of the clothesline. Drape the loops on the mantel until they are the length you want.

- Wrap the clothesline pieces with floral tape to help conceal them. Lay pieces on a table, and begin to wire on sprigs of evergreen, dried flower, pine cones, or whatever else complements your decorating scheme. Other attractive items include nuts, cotton balls, okra pods, milkweed pods, sweetgum balls, rose hips, chinaberries, magnolia leaves, pomegranates, other fruits.

- Attach pieces to nails, making sure both swags arc even. Attach bows either at the three nails or at the bottom of the two swags.

# Cone Tree Centerpieces

*P*opular in England for many centuries as a presentation for fresh fruit at the table, these nail-studded forms now serve mainly as decorative centerpieces and table adornments for the holidays.

## Materials

**Nail-studded cone**
**Greenery**
**Apples, lemons, oranges, or your choice**
**Leaves**
**Cardboard circle for base**

ᕙ Purchase a nail-studded cone from a crafts store, or make one from a wooden or Styrofoam cone. Place individual headless nails around the cone, with a few at the top.

ᕙ Skewer fruit on the nails on the tree, placing the larger pieces at the bottom and the smaller pieces closer to the top. Save the very largest piece for the top, or even use a different fruit at the top. If you vary the fruits on the tree, you can place each selection in a single row horizontally or vertically. Be consistent regarding stem placement.

ᕙ Add holly or boxwood sprigs to fill in the spaces between the fruits. Add attractive leaves to the edges of the cardboard circle, and center the cone on the circle. Place tree flat on a table or raise it on a cakestand.

# Lighting A Wreath

*W*reaths hang as attractive holiday adornments, but when the day darkens, a festive wreath gets lost in winter's night. The following idea allows you to "light" your wreath. By adding electric twinkle lights to any wreath, you get a glowing decoration for your door, window, or dark exterior wall. If you use battery-operated lights, you can add a glowing wreath to your car, doghouse, or street post. A lighted, glowing *wreath—what a welcome sight on a cold, dark winter night.*

- Wrap the light strands around the grapevine wreath. You may occasionally plug in the wreath to see if you have enough lights to suit you.

- Wire them in place if they aren't wrapped tightly enough.

- Use an extension cord to reach the closest outlet.

- Decorate the wreath as you would normally to match your holiday decor.

## Materials

Grapevine wreath
Several strands of clear mini twinkle lights
Extension cord
Wire

# Bows

*ow much do you spend on bows each year? You need bows for the wreaths, for the mailbox, for the swags and banisters, and for the packages. It can get expensive. This year try making your own professional-looking bows. It's really not that difficult.*

- 1. Make a loop with the ribbon to the size bow you want.

- 2. Loop and twist the ribbon completely at the center of each loop. Hold the center with one hand, and loop and twist with the other until you use the 5 yards of ribbon.

- 3. Tie the center securely with the wire. Use the extra ends of the wire to secure to the wreath other decorations.

## Materials

for wreath-size bow:
5 yards of stiff ribbon
12 inches of 20-gauge wire

- 4. Shape the loops with your fingers until bow is symmetrical and looks like you want. This same process can be done with smaller bows using less ribbon and wire.

# Stretching Your Fall Wreath

Start in fall with a 12- or 18-inch grapevine wreath. Collect pine cones, seed pods, acorns, small nuts, dried berries, wheat heads, pomegranates, etc. Picture your wreath with a clock face. At 12, 3, and 9, group your dried materials leaving about a 3-inch space at 2, 4, 8, and 10. For design purposes try to use the same selections at 12, 3, and 9, and hot glue onto the wreath. Tie a bow of plaid or fall color ribbons at 6 o'clock .

December 1st, remove the bow, and spray gold paint on the entire wreath. When dry, add bunches of evergreens and/or holly that have been wired together on a 3-inch wooden floral pick. Tuck into the spaces at 2, 4, 8, and 10. Place the bunches of evergreens in one direction around the wreath. Now add your Christmas bow at 6 o'clock. When using fresh evergreens, remember to hammer the end of the stems, and place in tepid water to harden for a day ahead before placing them on the wreath. Fresh greenery lasts about four weeks on an outside wreath.

# Greenery Plaque

Instead of the usual wreath for your porch, garden gate, or mailbox, try a greenery plaque with a foam cage. Floral foam cages are easily available in craft shops or from your florist. They come with a handle for easy hanging either indoors or out.

Soak the foam holder in water. Cut the stems of the greenery at an angle, and insert them around the outside edge of the foam plaque. Soak ivy, holly, pine, or any of the evergreens for several hours to retain freshness.

You will need a small supply of green floral picks to attach the remaining additions to your plaque. Dried cones, lotus pods,

pomegranates, and dried yarrow provide interesting additions. Fill spaces with more fresh greens and berries. Be sure your greenery is placed at different heights and going in different directions to achieve a graceful effect. You can always add a holiday bow if you would like.

◎

# Silver Bowl Centerpiece

In your favorite silver bowl (or a china bowl or basket), place a lace-edged napkin (or stitch a row of lace on a square of white fabric), leaving its four corners hanging over the edges. Fill your bowl with cinnamon sticks, whole cloves, small cones, nuts, and sprigs of herbs, such as rosemary, sage, thyme, roses, artemisia, and lamb's ears. Dried slices of oranges and apples lend color and scent too. Add sprigs of pine, cedar, or holly, and 4 drops of rose oil and 1 drop of cinnamon oil. Refresh the evergreens occasionally, or add a few gilded pomegranates to dramatize your arrangement. The fabric absorbs the odors and prolongs the scents from your fresh potpourri.

# New Year's Potpourri

*ave some of your holiday greens (pine, spruce, cedar, fir, etc.) that you used in your decorations, and dry them so you can enjoy the rest of the winter as a "Christmas Memory."*

In a large bowl place the following:

- 1 quart dried evergreens needles
- 2 cups dried flowers (roses and yarrow dry well)
- Dried cranberries or juniper berries
- Dried small cones or nuts
- Broken cinnamon sticks
- Dried orange or lemon peels
- 1 tablespoon each of cinnamon, whole cloves, allspice, and orris root (1 cup of oak moss can be used instead of orris root)
- 1½ teaspoons Christmas- or fir-scented oil

Mix well; fill a glass or pottery bowl or a large brandy snifter with the mixture. Potpourri adds decor to the room, a delightful fragrance for the winter months, and the warm memories of past holiday.

# Tablecloth Fancies

To create a layered "lacy petticoat" effect for your dining or side table, layer three or four tablecloths and lace. Select tablecloths in various sizes, colors, and styles to create the effect. For Christmas, for example, layer a cloth of red or green on your table. Then add a layer of lace (from fabric or upholstery shops) slightly smaller than the first cloth. Next, add a holiday plaid cloth smaller than the lace layer. To finish off, run a piece of lace runner and a Christmas ribbon down the length of the table. To get this same effect with a round table, you can use both square and round cloths.

# Snowman

*G*race your kitchen counter with Mr. Snowman. You can fill him with popcorn or marshmallows or anything that's light in color so it shows up well.

- For top hat, cut one piece of cardboard 4 inches by 12½ inches; roll and glue together to make chimney. Glue felt on chimney.

- For the brim, cut out a round piece of cardboard with a 7¼-inch diameter; cover with felt on both sides. Glue chimney to brim. Circle the hat with a 20-inch length of ribbon; tie, and decorate with a Christmas pin or decoration.

- The body of the snowman is two fish bowls. Use five round black felt cutouts for eyes and buttons. Make eyebrows out of black felt. Use red felt for the nose and mouth. Highlight the eyes and buttons with white felt.

- Fill bowls with popcorn or whatever you may desire. Place small fish bowl on top of large one. Add 24 inches of 1-inch-wide ribbon for the scarf; decorate with a candy cane. Top Mr. Snowman with his hat.

## Materials

Cardboard
Felt—black, white, and red
Ribbon
Glue
1 (6-inch) fish bowl
1 (5-inch) fish bowl
Christmas pin or decoration
Candy cane

# Cinnamon Spice

or an easy festive touch to your home, purchase a container of cinnamon. Place the cinnamon sticks in table arrangements and wreaths. Take four or five cinnamon sticks, clustering them in a bunch. Tie with a holiday ribbon or bow. Cinnamon clusters can be placed on top of books, in a guestroom or bath, by the telephone— any place you want to add a touch of color and aroma.

For an unusual and practical trivet, wire cinnamon sticks together in a star shape. When a hot pot is placed on the star, the fragrance of cinnamon is released. Use copper or noncorrosive wire. Make trivets to fit any size pan or casserole dish by altering the lengths of wire and cinnamon sticks.

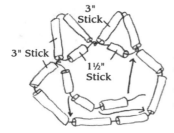

**3" Stick**

**3" Stick**

**1½" Stick**

Attach one end of 11" wire (strung with 1½" sticks between two 3" sticks. Continue wiring between 3" sticks, forming triangles with one 1½" stick and two 3" sticks.

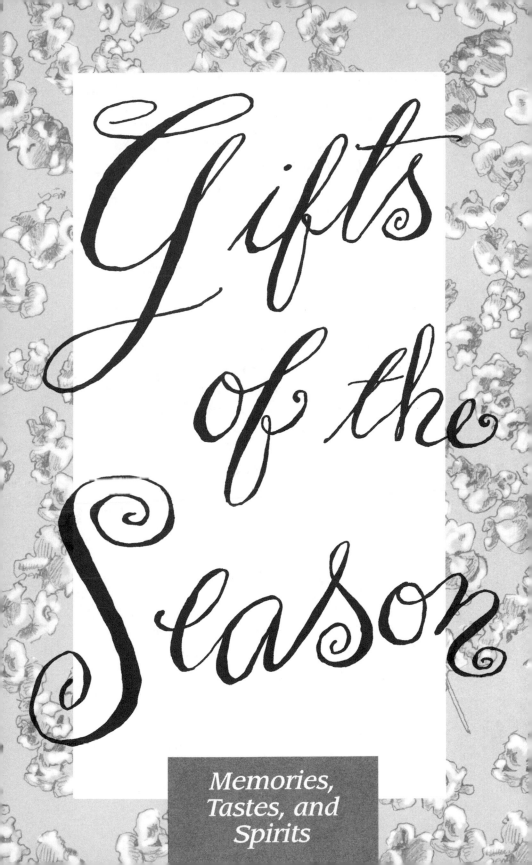

# Gifts of the Season

**Memories, Tastes, and Spirits**

*T*here is no other aspect of the holiday season that creates more anxiety than selecting the right gifts for friends and family. If your budget is tight and the list is long, review the ideas in this chapter.

Gift giving is an art, and its practice need not break your bank account or drain your energy. Giving of yourself is one of the greatest holiday gifts.

A gift of food from your kitchen is always appreciated. People who do not have the time or talent to cook, look forward to a gift of Christmas candy or bread as much, if not more, than a store-bought present.

If you are into crafts, our ideas for Christmas jewelry will add a new dimension to your gift giving.

If both crafts and cooking are out, don't be alarmed. We have included ideas for you ranging from gifts of forced bulbs to more than 10 gift basket ideas for everyone on your list.

As each gift is unique, so are our ideas for packaging and presenting the gifts. A quick trip to a crafts store for holiday ribbons, supplies, and a glue gun should get you on your way.

Don't wait until the week before Christmas to find unique bottles, jars, boxes, and packaging for your gifts; make this a year-round adventure. In the heat of a July yard sale, you are likely to find just the perfect antique tea cup to include with a spiced tea mix.

A simple item like a bottle of wine becomes a unique gift when a miniature grapevine holiday wreath is added to the decor. Peppermint marshmallows in holiday shapes add a new twist to cocoa mix.

The art of gift giving is limited only by the creativity of the giver. Use our ideas to jump-start your creativity to ensure a unique gift-giving season.

# Gift Baskets

*G*ift baskets are one of the nicest personal gifts you can give at the holidays. Create a gift basket based on the gift receiver's hobbies, favorite foods, or fantasies.

Package the gift items in a basket filled with shredded paper. Place the items artistically. Wrap the package in clear cellophane, and tie a bow at the top. Some of the gifts, such as the watering can in the gardener basket, could be used as the container. If you find baskets a bit pricey, use a beautiful gift bag filled with colorful tissue paper.

The great thing these gifts provide is that personal touch to match someone's interest—and to keep within your budget.

## Artist

Calligraphy pens
Drawing pad
Gift certificate for framing
Watercolors and markers
Tickets to an art exhibit
or museum

## Athlete

Socks
Weights
Ticket to sporting events
Sports hats, sweatshirts
Athletic bag

## Bookworm

Bestseller
Bookmarks
Book embosser
Gift certificate
Magazines
Book on tape

## Baker

Cookie cutters
Mini muffin pan
Spice organizer
Cookbook
Recipe cards/file box

## Chocoholic

Gourmet chocolate chips

Box of truffles

Hot fudge sauce

Unique chocolate shapes

Gourmet hot cocoa mixes

## Coffee Lover

Mug

Sampler of foreign coffee

Gift certificate to a coffee shop

Permanent coffee filter

Espresso pot

Espresso cups and spoons

## Gardener

Seed packets

Gardening gloves

Watering can

Gardening knee pads

Garden tools

## Hostess

Pretty napkins and rings

Candles

Liqueur

Guest towels

Decorative wine stopper

Coasters

## Pasta Lover

Flavored pasta

Gourmet olive oil

Pasta cookbook

Pasta bowl

Pasta server

# Framed Photos

*mall framed photos made into ornaments provide grandparent gifts that are much appreciated. If attached with ribbons, they are perfect to decorate the grandparents' tree.*

- Purchase small, inexpensive brass or plastic picture frames.

- Ask family members to provide individual photos of each family member—Polaroids work fine.

- Cut the photos to fit the frames.

- Attach each frame with a festive holiday ribbon.

- Present grandparents with new holiday ornaments—pictures of all family members. Photos can be updated each year.

# A Gift for the Birds

*f you'd like to teach your children to appreciate and respect nature, have them give the birds a Christmas gift—their own tree. This can be done as a party for neighborhood children or a Sunday afternoon activity for just your clan!*

If you have a tree in the yard that's close to a window, you can decorate it. If you want a "real" tree, ensure that the base is sturdy enough to handle the weight of the ornaments and the kids pulling branches down to place the treats.

*(Continued on page 32)*

# Bird Lanterns

*6 yards of 18-gauge florist wire*
*12 pine cones*
*3 pounds peanut butter*
*1½ pounds suet*
*10 pounds birdseed*

Twist the florist wire around the large end of the pine cone, and make a hook at the end. Mix peanut butter and suet. Spread the peanut butter mixture on the pine cones. Roll the pine cones in a large bowl of birdseed.

# Popcorn, Pretzels, and Cranberry Garlands

Just as you would for you own tree, use wire or thread and create different garlands.

# Sweet Treats

*12 powdered doughnuts*
*12 cinnamon doughnuts*
*8 yards (¼-inch-wide) ribbon*

Cut ribbon into 12-inch lengths. Loop ribbon through doughnuts; tie in a knot.

# Bird Tree Ornaments

*1 loaf of stale bread*
*Christmas ornament hangers*

Using your Christmas cookie cutters, cut each slice of bread into the desired shape. Hang on the tree with ornament hangers.

# Fruit Cup Baskets

*12 oranges*
*3 cups birdseed*
*3 cups suet*
*3 cups sunflower seeds*
*3 cups raisins*
*12 feet (¹⁄₂-inch-wide) ribbon*

Cut oranges into a basket shape. Scoop out pulp. Mix the ingredients together, and place inside each basket. Loop ribbon through each basket handle to hang on tree.

# Small Family Cookbook

*ere's a gift idea to preserve cherished family recipes without spending much money or time.*

- Ask family members to send you their favorite recipes.

- Divide an 8½ x 11-inch piece of paper into quarters.

- Type or print each recipe so that it fits into one quarter of a page.

- Copy the recipes on card stock paper (one set of recipes for each gift) and cut them into quarters.

- Hole punch the recipes in the upper lefthand corner

- Design a cover for your family cookbook.

- Insert the ring.

*(Continued on page 34)*

## Materials

Favorite family recipes
Typewriter or pen
Loose-leaf binder rings
Hole punch

Note: A simple thing to do is go to your neighborhood copy center. Ask them to laminate your cover design on the front and back. Ask them to copy your recipes on card stock. They have the equipment to perfectly cut your recipes, and hole punch them for you.

# Holiday Jewelry

*Don't shy away from these ideas even if you are not "crafty." All you need is a quick trip to your crafts store, a glue gun, and your imagination. You can make 50 pairs of earrings for less than $10.*

## Christmas Earrings

*1 package of earring loops or clasps*
*( they are sold 25 sets to a package)*
*2 packages of miniature Christmas ornaments*
*with a hook/loop*
*(Look at your crafts store in the section that sells items for small trees or Christmas villages.)*

↬ Take a set of earring hooks. Open the end and thread on a Christmas light, Christmas ball, or bell. Voilà, an instant gift.

↬ If you are feeling very crafty, you can make tiny bows and glue them on at the connection.

## Christmas Pendant

*Pin backs*
*A variety of miniature ornaments*
*A clear 1-inch button, or a color of your choice*
*Ribbons*
*Greenery*
*Gold cording*
*Glue gun*

- Glue the largest or your favorite ornament in the center.

- Surround with smaller ornaments.

- Add ribbons, cording, or greenery to fill in.

## Reindeer Pin

*Large dog biscuits that have been spray-shellacked*
*Glitter pipe cleaners*
*Doll eyes*
*Pin back (from hobby store)*
*Small red pom-poms for the nose*

- Use dog biscuits as the face. With a glue gun add reindeer eyes and nose.

- Cut pipe cleaners in half, and bend to form antlers. Glue to dog biscuit.

- Glue pin on back of biscuit.

## Flowering Bulbs

*To receive a gift that is blooming during the holiday season pleases many gift recipients. Giving a hyacinth bulb and glass, amaryllis, or paperwhites makes an easy inexpensive present. You can time forcing your bulbs so that they will bloom during the dark, dreary days of January.*

- In the fall, purchase bulbs at a garden center or hardware store. Place the bulbs in your refrigerator for at least three weeks.

- When ready to prepare the gift, rinse the gravel several times to remove the white dust.

### Materials

*Bulbs (amaryllis or paperwhites)*
*Shallow plastic or clay saucers (no holes)*
*Small bag white gravel*
*Corsage bags*
*Ribbon*

*(Continued on page 36)*

Place bulbs in a corsage bag (5 to 6 bulbs will fill the saucer). Place gravel in a separate corsage bag. Tie both bags with a festive ribbon, and place in the saucer.

Include the following instructions: *Place gravel in saucer, position bulbs pointed up in gravel, and fill in gravel around them. Fill the saucer with water until it touches the bottom of the bulbs. Set the container in a dark cool spot. When roots develop in two to three weeks, move the pot to a sunny but cool spot. Shoots will develop rapidly, and in about three weeks you'll have masses of fragrant flowers.*

For hyacinths, place bulbs in the refrigerator for three to five weeks. Purchase hyacinth forcing vases at your garden center. Place one bulb into the vase, pointing up. Wrap the vase and bulb in cellophane, and tie with a beautiful holiday ribbon. Include the following instructions: *Fill the vase with water until it reaches the base of the bulb. In about 1 month, you will have a beautiful, fragrant hyacinth blossom.*

# Mini Grapevine Wreaths

*Use these tiny wreaths on the neck of a wine bottle or around the bottom of small candlesticks when you give these gifts to friends or relatives.*

Starting at the top of the mini wreath and moving in a clockwise motion, decorate these small 3-inch wreaths with no more that an inch tip from boxwood, Japanese holly, or rosemary; glue them on the wreath using a hot glue gun. (If you use rosemary, it is the Christmas herb and means remembrance.) Add small dried flowers, berries, or hemlock cones occasionally on top of the greenery or even tiny gold ribbon bows can be attached.

# That Christmasy Smell

*P*lace 4 large cinnamon sticks, 2 teaspoons ground allspice, 1 fresh gingerroot, 20 whole cloves, and 2 tablespoons pickling spices in a decorative jar. This is a wonderful gift to give someone to help them achieve that Christmasy smell in their home. Attach a card that reads: *I've gathered these spices just for you. There's one thing now that you must do. Pour these spices in a kettle or pot; add a quart of water and cook until hot. Now turn the heat down low and simmer for a while. Your house will smell Christmasy and bring lots of smiles.* (This is not for consumption.)

# Macaroni Angels

*Children will love to make these with you to give as gifts to friends and teachers.*

## Materials

for one angel:
1 rigatoni noodle
Glue
3/4-inch wooden bead
Soup macaronis
1 bow tie pasta
2 elbow macaronis
White acrylic spray
Gold thread
Gold fine-tipped permanent marker
Miniature decoration

- Glue wooden bead to top of rigatoni. Glue soup macaronis to top of head to make hair.

- Glue bow tie pasta to back of angel for wings. For arms, glue elbow macaronis to front of angel.

- Spray angel with acrylic paint.

- Make hanger out of gold thread through a soup macaroni on tip of head. Knot ends to form a loop.

- Draw eyes on with marker. Glue miniature decoration between arms.

# Play Dough

*P*lay dough is a great gift for children. Guaranteed to fill an afternoon with fun. Package in small cans with lids. Tie a ribbon around each.

## Materials

1 cup all-purpose flour
½ cup salt
1 cup water
1 tablespoon oil
2 teaspoons cream of tartar
Food coloring

Combine all ingredients except food coloring. Cook and stir in saucepan over medium heat until mixture forms a ball (about 3 minutes). Remove from heat. Divide dough, and color each section as desired. Knead several minutes on wax paper until dough is smooth and workable and color is consistent.

# Dog Treats

*I*f a dog is man's best friend, then Fido deserves his own holiday gift. Package dog biscuits in a large jar. Include a copy of the recipe and a dog bone cookie cutter so Fido's master can make some too.

## Materials

1½ cups cooked, skinned, deboned chicken
2 tablespoons chicken broth
1 egg
1 tablespoon chopped parsley
1 teaspoon garlic powder
1 cup yellow cornmeal
2 tablespoons coarsely crumbled fiber cereal
½ cup whole wheat flour

Purée first 3 ingredients in blender. Pour into large bowl, and add parsley and garlic. Stir well, cover, and refrigerate overnight.

On a floured surface, roll out dough to ¼ inch thick. Using dog treat cookie cutter, cut into treats. Place about ½-inch apart on greased baking sheet. Bake at 350° for 15 to 20 minutes. Remove from oven, and cool on pans. Refrigerate treats in airtight container for up to 2 weeks or freeze for longer storage.

*Homemade Christmas*

# Food Gifts

## Dried Orange & Lemon Peel

To dry peels, preheat oven to 150°. Peel oranges and lemons, saving only outermost peeling. Cut into strips (3x½-inch). Place on baking sheet in single layer, and bake for 2 hours or until slices are crisp and dry. Yield: 8 orange peel slices; 8 lemon peel slices.

These are wonderful inexpensive gifts. Take several medium jars, wash and dry them, and fill with the dried peels. Seal tightly. To decorate, cut circles of fabric 1 inch larger than your jar top. Using gold cord or raffia, tie the fabric to the jar top. These are great when added to hot cider along with cinnamon and cloves.

## Cranberry-Walnut Conserve

*Tie jar with a ribbon, and attach a note card (and recipe card, if you care to share).*

**1 pound cranberries**
**1 cup water**
**2 cups sugar**
**Juice and grated rind of 1 orange**
**Juice and grated rind of 1 lemon or lime**
**2 cups coarsely broken walnuts or pecans**
**1 cup golden raisins**
**½ cup dry wine**

Combine cranberries and water in a saucepan, and bring to a boil; reduce heat, and simmer 3 to 4 minutes or until cranberries pop. Add

*(Continued on page 40)*

sugar and juice and rind of orange and lemon; simmer about 15 minutes longer, stirring occasionally. Remove from heat, and stir in walnuts, raisins, and wine. Pour into attractive jars and seal.

**YIELD: 2 TO 2½ PINTS**

## Lynn's Divinity

*An old tray or glass plate will finish this gift idea. Do not let the divinity touch. Wrap the tray in colored plastic wrap, and add an inexpensive holiday ornament or bow.*

**2½ cups granulated sugar**
**½ cup light corn syrup**
**¼ teaspoon salt**
**½ cup water**
**2 egg whites**
**1 teaspoon vanilla**

In a 2-quart saucepan, combine sugar, corn syrup, salt, and water. Cook to hard boil stage (260°) stirring only until sugar dissolves. Meanwhile, beat egg whites at high speed on electric mixer until stiff peaks form. Add sugar mixture and vanilla, and beat until candy holds its shape, 4 to 5 minutes. Quickly drop teaspoonsful onto waxed paper.

**YIELD: 40 SERVINGS**

## Irish Cream Whiskey

*At your local craft, hobby, or cooking stores, purchase inexpensive clear bottles. Decorate with a holiday ribbon.*

**3 egg yolks**
**1 (14-ounce) can sweetened condensed milk**
**1¼ cups whipping cream**
**1½ cups whiskey**
**1½ tablespoons chocolate syrup**
**¼ teaspoon coconut extract**

$\mathcal{I}$n a large bowl beat egg yolks until thick. Stir in condensed milk, whipping cream, whiskey, chocolate syrup, and coconut extract. Beat for 1 minute. Pour mixture into a large decanter; store in the refrigerator. Let mellow 7 days.

YIELD: 1 GIFT

# Lemon Curd

$\mathcal{S}$mall jam jars, new or recycled, are perfect packages for this delicious gift.

**1 cup sugar**
**¼ cup butter**
**Grated peel of two lemons**
**Juice of three lemons**
**3 eggs, beaten**

In a bowl or double boiler placed over a saucepan of hot water, combine sugar, butter, lemon peel, and lemon juice. Place over low heat. Cook until butter melts, stirring occasionally. Stir in eggs, do not let mixture boil or it will curdle. Continue stirring over heat until mixture thickens. Pour into jars. Store in refrigerator.

YIELD: 1 GIFT

# Coffee Liqueur

$\mathcal{A}$t flea markets and garage sales, look for old liquor bottles, wash them well, and fill with liqueur. You can also find decorative bottles at craft stores.

**2 cups water**
**4½ cups sugar**
**4 teaspoons instant coffee**
**Drop vanilla extract**
**1 cup brandy**
**1 cup rum**

(Continued on page 42)

*I*n a saucepan, combine water, sugar, coffee, and vanilla. Heat gently, stirring until sugar and coffee have dissolved. Cool. Stir brandy and rum into syrup. Pour into a decanter, and seal. Allow to mellow two to three weeks.

**YIELD: 1 SERVING**

# Herb Butter

*P*ackage these butters in decorative crocks or ramekins. Include a holiday spreader or loaf of bread as part of the gift.

**1 cup butter**
**1 teaspoon each parsley, sage, oregano,**
**and rosemary, chopped**

Beat butter until creamy. Add herbs, and beat again. Roll into cylinders and cover with plastic wrap. Refrigerate.

To make basil butter, add 10 to12 minced basil leaves to ½ cup butter. For garlic butter, add 2 tablespoons minced garlic to ½ cup butter and any other favorite herb.

**YIELD: 1 GIFT**

# Caramel Sauce

*P*our into a pint canning jar, and add a holiday ribbon at the neck of the jar. Attach an ice cream scoop to accompany the gift.

**½ cup brown sugar**
**¾ cup sugar**
**⅓ cup butter**
**½ cup light corn syrup**
**⅔ cup whipping cream**

In a saucepan, combine all ingredients except whipping cream. Cook over medium heat, stirring until mixture comes to a full boil.

Cool five minutes.  Stir in whipping cream.  Store in refrigerator.

**YIELD:  1 GIFT**

# Chocolate Spoons

*ackage 12 of these spoons in a coffee mug with the Mocha Coffee Mix as a gift for a special teacher. The spoons serve as tasty stirrers for coffee or hot chocolate.*

**6 ounces semisweet chocolate**

**3 ounces white chocolate**

**12 heavy plastic spoons**

In a skillet place one inch of water; bring to a boil.  Reduce heat.  In a 2 cup measuring cup place the semisweet chocolate; place cup in skillet.  In 1 cup measure place white chocolate; add cup to skillet.  Stir each 5 to 10 minutes until melted.  Dip spoon into chocolate.  Drizzle white chocolate on spoons, using a toothpick swirl white chocolate to create a marbleized look.  Set spoons on wax paper until room temperature.

**YIELD:  12 SPOONS**

# Peanut Butter Fudge

*our the fudge into small aluminum loaf pans with lids; include a plastic knife for cutting.*

**2 cups sugar**

**⅔ cup evaporated milk**

**7 ounces marshmallow cream**

**1 cup peanut butter**

Boil sugar and milk 6 minutes.  Start slowly so sugar will be dissolved.  Remove from heat.  Add marshmallow cream and peanut butter.  Beat until blended and begins to thicken.  Pour into a lightly

*(Continued on page 44)*

buttered 9 x 9-inch pan.  Cool and slice.

**YIELD:  40 SERVINGS**

# Creamy Creole Pralines

*rap each praline in plastic wrap, and place in a tall cookie tin. Add a holiday or raffia bow.*

*1 cup sugar*

*1 cup dark brown sugar*

*2 tablespoons light corn syrup*

*½ cup half-and-half*

*2 teaspoons butter*

*1 teaspoon vanilla*

*1 cup pecan pieces*

In a saucepan dissolve the sugars and syrup in the half-and-half over medium heat.  Bring the mixture to a boil, and continue cooking until a candy thermometer registers 228°, stirring occasionally.

Add the butter, vanilla, and pecans; cook until 236°, and then remove from the heat. Cool the candy to 225°, and beat until thickened. Drop by tablespoons onto wax paper, working rapidly.

The candy will flatten out. When cool, wrap in wax paper, and store in a covered container.

**YIELD:  12 SERVINGS**

# Chocolate Truffles

*egin saving the boxes your checks come in. Wrap them in an elegant foil holiday wrap. Place plastic in the bottom of the box. Add the truffles. Tie the box in a beautiful holiday ribbon.*

*9 ounces semisweet chocolate, cut up*

*½ cup whipping cream*

*½ cup unsalted butter*
*2 egg yolks, beaten*
*Chopped nuts, powdered sugar, cocoa*
*and/or flaked coconut*

❧ In a heavy saucepan combine chocolate and cream. Cook over low heat until chocolate melts. Add the butter, cook and stir until butter melts. Slowly stir about half the hot mixture into egg yolks; then return mixture to saucepan. Cook and stir over medium heat until mixture comes to a gentle boil. Remove from heat. Chill in refrigerator 3 to 4 hours or until firm. Once cool, spoon up about 2 teaspoons chocolate mixture; roll into a ball. Roll in coating of your choice. Refrigerate until serving time.

**YIELD: 1 GIFT**

# Chocolate Turtles

*A t a local candy or bakery supply store, purchase candy boxes with the liners. Make a tag with your name followed by Candy Shop. Your friends will think you've gone into business.*

*1  pound caramels*
*2 tablespoons water*
*3 cups pecan halves*
*12 ounces chocolate chips*

❧ In the top of a double boiler, melt the caramels. Add the water and pecans, stirring until the nuts are evenly distributed. Using a teaspoon, drop the candy on wax paper, and let cool. In a double boiler melt the chocolate chips. Spoon chocolate over the candy.

**YIELD: 24 SERVINGS**

# Almond Brittle

*Package these in candy tins or on an inexpensive glass plate.*

1 cup sugar

⅔ cup white corn syrup

½ cup water

1 cup slivered almonds

1 teaspoon baking soda

1 teaspoon vanilla

1 teaspoon butter

Cook sugar, corn syrup, and water until it reaches hard crack stage. (Mixture will separate into hard brittle threads.) Add almonds, stirring constantly. Cook until syrup is golden in color. Remove from heat; Add soda, vanilla, and butter. Stir until butter melts. Pour mixture into buttered pan and let harden.

**YIELD: 16 SERVINGS**

# Peppermint Liqueur

*At your local crafts, hobby, or cooking store, purchase inexpensive clear bottles. Add a holiday ribbon.*

1 cup water

2 cups sugar

1 teaspoon peppermint extract

1½ cups brandy

½ teaspoon green food coloring

In a saucepan, combine water and sugar; stir gently on low heat until sugar dissolves. Cool. Stir in peppermint extract, brandy, and enough food color to make the syrup the color of creme de menthe. Pour into a sterilized bottle. Mellow seven days.

**YIELD: 1 GIFT**

# Pesto

*am jars, new or recycled, are perfect containers for this gift. For the pasta lover, include tree or star-shaped pasta and a pasta server.*

**¾ cup walnuts**

**3 cups stemmed basil leaves**

**1 ½ cups olive oil**

**1 cup Parmesan cheese**

**4 medium cloves garlic**

Put ingredients in a food processor or blender. Turn the machine on and off rapidly. Pulse the ingredients several times until coarsely chopped. Scrape down the work bowl. Process again until the mixture is smooth. Add additional olive oil if mixture is too thick.

**YIELD: 6 SERVINGS**

# Sugar & Spice Pecans

*am jars or holiday tins become perfect containers for these tasty pecans.*

**1 cup brown sugar**

**3 tablespoons evaporated milk**

**1 tablespoon butter**

**1 teaspoon orange peel**

**2 cups pecan halves**

In small saucepan, combine the sugar and evaporated milk. Cook over medium heat to 234° (soft-ball stage), stirring occasionally. Add butter and orange peel; stir to blend. Add pecan halves, and stir to coat. Spread on parchment paper or a greased cookie sheet. When candy coating is firm, gently break pecans apart.

**YIELD: 4 SERVINGS**

# Caramels

*These should be packaged in a single layer. Give a decorative plate as part of the gift or place in a candy box.*

**1 pint whipping cream**

**1¾ cups light corn syrup**

**2 cups sugar**

**¾ cup butter**

**1 teaspoon vanilla**

**1 cup chopped nuts**

Mix cream, syrup, sugar, and butter in a heavy saucepan. Cook until 246° to 248° on a candy thermometer. Remove from heat, and beat in vanilla. Pour over chopped nuts that have been put in a 9 x 9-inch pan. Cool and cut into squares.

**YIELD: 24 SERVINGS**

# Merry Mocha Mix

*Pack mix in jars. For a special gift basket, add 1 jar of Merry Mocha Mix, 1 bag of marshmallows, and 1 or 2 cinnamon sticks or Chocolate Spoons (page 43). Attach a note card that reads: "Add 3 to 4 tablespoons of Merry Mocha Mix to ¾ cup boiling water. Stir until dissolved. Top with marshmallows or whipped cream. Stir with a cinnamon stick."*

**2 cups unsweetened cocoa**

**4 cups non-dairy creamer (powder)**

**5 cups sugar**

**4 cups nonfat dry milk**

**1 cup instant coffee**

**2 vanilla beans, cut into quarters**

Pour first 5 ingredients in large bowl, and stir until well blended. Pack in jars, and add a quartered piece of vanilla bean to each jar.

Store in refrigerator for at least 6 to 8 weeks before using to allow mocha mix to absorb vanilla.

YIELD: 8 PINT JARS

# Instant Spicy Tea in a Jar

*Pack in pint jars. Attach a copy of gift card, ribbon, and a cinnamon stick to each individual jar of spicy tea. Package with an antique cup and saucer, if desired. Note card should read: "To one cup of boiling water, add 2 to 3 teaspoons of the mix. Then stir your hot spiced tea with cinnamon sticks."*

**1 (18-ounce) jar powdered orange drink mix**

**2¼ cups sugar**

**2 teaspoons cinnamon**

**1 cup instant tea**

**1 teaspoon cloves**

**1 (4.6-ounce) package powdered lemonade**

Mix all ingredients, and store in airtight jars.

YIELD: 4 PINT JARS

# Red Hot Pepper Jelly

*Pack in jars, tie with ribbon, and package with spreader and crackers.*

**6 large red peppers, seeded and chopped**

**1 (4-ounce) can chopped jalapeño peppers, drained**

**1½ cups cider vinegar**

**1½ cups apple juice**

**2 (1¾-ounce) packages dry fruit pectin**

**¾ teaspoon salt**

**5 cups sugar**

*(Continued on page 50)*

Process red peppers, jalapeño peppers, and vinegar in blender until puréed. Add apple juice, cover, and let stand overnight. Strain through cheesecloth. Combine 4 cups pepper juice, pectin, and salt. Bring to rolling boil. Add 5 cups of sugar, dissolve, and return to rolling boil. Continue boiling for 1 minute. Remove from heat, and skim foam. Pour into jelly jars, and seal.

**YIELD: 6 HALF-PINT JARS**

## Remoulade Sauce

*A jam jar is a perfect container for this delicious sauce.*

**1 cup mayonnaise**
**1 tablespoon chopped onion**
**1 1/2 tablespoons chopped parsley**
**2 tablespoons Dijon mustard**
**1 tablespoon horseradish**
**1 teaspoon paprika**
**1/2 teaspoon salt**
**1 tablespoon vinegar**
**1 tablespoon Worcestershire sauce**
**1/2 cup salad oil**

Combine all ingredients except oil; add oil slowly. Refrigerate.

**YIELD: 1 JAR**

## Fantasy Fudge

*Pour fudge into holiday aluminum baking pans that have lids. Add a plastic green or red knife for cutting, place lid, and wrap with a festive bow. This will be your chocoholic's dream—an uncut pan of fudge.*

**3/4 cup margarine**
**3 cups sugar**
**2/3 cup evaporated milk**

*12 ounces semisweet chocolate chips*
*1 jar marshmallow cream*
*1 cup chopped nuts*
*1 teaspoon vanilla*

Mix margarine, sugar, and milk in a heavy 2½-to 3-quart saucepan; bring to a full boil, stirring constantly. Continue boiling 5 minutes over medium heat or until candy thermometer reaches 234°, stirring constantly to prevent scorching. Remove from heat. Gradually stir in chips until melted. Add remaining ingredients; mix well. Pour into a greased 9-inch square pan. Cool at room temperature.

**YIELD: 24 SERVINGS**

# In the Spirit of the Season

*ake the holiday season to teach your children that the true meaning of Christmas comes in giving of oneself and not always being the recipient. Following are a list of ideas for your family to participate in during the season:*

◉ When selecting gifts for their friends, have each child pick a gift for a mystery child—someone who might not be receiving gifts. Have the child donate the gift to a charity drive.

◉ Help an elderly neighbor decorate his or her home—and be sure there is food in the pantry.

◉ Offer to take an elderly neighbor to church for Christmas music.

◉ Invite that new family in the neighborhood over for cookies and cocoa.

◉ Organize a holiday party for a nursing home

◉ Help at a soup kitchen during the holidays.

◉ Adopt a family from a homeless shelter for the season. Help make sure they have the essentials and a few happy items.

*(Continued on page 52)*

- Instead of giving presents, make a donation to your favorite charity in honor of everyone on your Christmas list.

- Have your children donate coats and sweaters that are too small to a charity.

- Organize or participate in a canned food drive.

- Offer to Christmas shop for someone who is ill or house bound.

- Visit a relative you haven't seen in a while.

- Offer baby sitting services to someone who can't afford a sitter.

- Offer tickets to a Christmas play to a young family you know couldn't afford them.

- Offer hugs and kisses to people who might not be receiving them this season.

- Tell a lot of people that you love them.

- Read Christmas stories at shelters or for shut-ins.

- Visit your church or synagogue, participate in singing, and remember the reason for the season.

*The greatest gift you can give is your time and your self.*

# Setting the Stage

## Menus and Entertaining

*H*oliday entertaining is much like a theater production. You are the director. Your guests are the stars. Your home, the food, and decorations set the stage. Included in this chapter are menus from folks from around the country and the memories associated with their menu suggestions. For example, a New England Christmas Eve supper, Cajun New Year's, and Northwest Holiday Brunch.

Seven great party ideas follow the regional menus—with ideas that you can use in total, or pick favorites of each and recipes to weave into your holiday entertaining. Each party idea offered in *Homemade Christmas* provides ideas for invitations, food, decorations, and favors. Putting these parties together will be a snap.

The party ideas in this chapter have been developed to serve as a guide—not a mandate. If you're thinking that your schedule doesn't allow for a party—think again. These ideas are not complicated. Concentrate on preparing one or two of the more lavish recipes—then pick up the rest of the menu items from a deli, bakery, or favorite restaurant. Never be embarrassed to fill in your party menus with commercially prepared products. Every item need not be homemade.

Always remember, your guests want to visit with you—enjoy the setting and atmosphere you've created, not the complexity of the food you served.

Happy entertaining!

# Cold Winter's Night Repast in New England

My beloved in-laws, Edna and Charles Allen, were known respectively as quite the hostess and baker in Hillsboro, New Hampshire, which is northwest of Manchester. Charles, one of American Airlines first captains, began baking when he retired. He even tried some of his baked goods in the wood stove of their old restored farmhouse. Edna was a jazz pianist who had her own band at one time and created the music for "Everyone Loves My Baby." The Allens entertained often—many times people just dropped by and they would feed them. This menu provides a wonderful warming welcome after church services on Christmas Eve. The recipes are directly from the Allens' files. The pie recipes have been handed down through several generations. The Sour Cream Pie was Included in a notebook from Charles' grandmother.

**Linda Merritt Allen**
*New Canaan, Connecticut*

## Menu

Quick
Bouillabaisse
page 114

Green Salad

Buttered Toast
Points

Sour Cream Pie
page 204

Squash Pie
page 205

*(Linda also shares Capt'n Allen's Anadama Bread found on page 104. Charles used to make this recipe and oatmeal bread for all the holidays, keeping the whole family in homemade bread all year long.)*

# Traditional Christmas Dinner — Ohio Style

**B**eing British by birth, my family and I always have tried to maintain some of the traditions of the old sod. Roast beef and Yorkshire pudding have long been family favorites on Christmas Day. I think we like it, too, because it requires very little work, leaving more time to spend with family and friends. We usually serve it with the accompaniments below, but sometimes we include acorn squash. You can choose the accompaniments that your family likes best.

A perfect ending for this British meal would be a Plum Pudding; however, this takes lots of preparation time—many days before the feast. We usually make Trifle, which consists of sponge cake or ladyfingers doused with spirits (usually sherry), covered with jam or custard, topped with whipped cream, and garnished with fruit, nuts, or chocolate.

*Peter D. Franklin*
*Columbus, Ohio*
*Syndicated Food Columnist*
*Universal Press Syndicate*

## Menu

**Roast Beef**
*page 114*

**Yorkshire Pudding**
*page 114*

**Peas**

**Parsnips**

**Turnips**

**Carrots**

**Plum Pudding**
*page 212*
*or Trifle*

# Cajun New Year's

If you believe in Acadian folklore, legend tells of *Le Petit Bonhomme Janvier,* the little man of January, who visits the homes of good little children (and sometimes adults) on New Year's Eve and brings small sacks of treats.

I learned about this little man on New Year's Eve when we children were farmed out to Nannan's so Mama and Papa could have a night on the town. Nannan had laid down plump quilts over the cold, hard wooden floors and turned up the gas heaters that burned brightly in the living room. There was no television then, so Nannan had tuned to WWL radio where music was coming "live and direct" from the Roosevelt Hotel's Blue Room in New Orleans.

Nannan had promised us a treat of hot chocolate with marshmallows and plates of cheese toast. Then we were sent off to the big four poster beds to sleep so that *Le Petit Bonhomme Janvier* could "make his pass" with his goodies.

Early the next morning, hung on the posters of the beds, was a sack for each of us, filled with "sussies" of all kinds—apples, oranges, mandarins, candied pecans, little dolls made out of clothespins, and pralines wrapped in red cellophane paper tied up with gold ribbons!

With our sacks and pajamas in hand, we were returned to Mama and Papa for a big New Year's Day celebration. To this day, the tradition still continues—as does the New Year's Day tradition of dining on black-eyed peas (for good luck) and cabbage (to ensure monetary success). It is not unusual to spend the day going from house to house to enjoy Milk Punches and Bloody Marys and, of course, having a taste of their black-eyed peas and cabbage. After all, more should be better. Who wouldn't want more luck or more monetary success in the New Year?

*Marcelle Bienvenu*
*St. Martinville, Louisiana*

## Menu

**Milk Punch**
*page 93*

**Bloody Marys**
*page 94*

**Black-eyed Peas**
*page 136*

**Smothered Cabbage**
*page 137*

**Glazed Ham**
*page 112*

# Traditional Southern Christmas

My husband's family, as well as my own, has its roots in Mississippi so there is a definite "Southern Bend" to our Christmas dinner. It has remained pretty much the same for as long as I can remember.

The cornbread always has to be made at least two days in advance to ensure "proper" drying. There has always been the ongoing debate about whether yellow or white cornmeal makes the best cornbread. The Osgood pies are always better if they can "age" a day or so as well. The trick is to keep someone from cutting them!

## Menu

We have always made our own cranberry sauce as well. We enjoy molding and garnishing it. The deep-red cranberry color always looks so festive.

A favorite dessert is a cake that my grandmother devised in the early thirties. We baked as many as 85 cakes during the holiday season and sold them. This ensured a much more bountiful Christmas during some lean Depression years. She built such a clientele that she continued baking them until the early seventies. The recipe has stayed with us and is a family favorite, particularly the caramel icing that covers it.

We've always stuffed our turkey, and everyone always wants the dressing that was "stuffed." We all swear that it tastes much better than the casserole baked dressing.

Ambrosia was always a staple for Christmas dinners, and somewhere along the way it began to be embellished with maraschino cherries, pecans, apples, pineapple, and bananas—and always served with fresh whipped cream.

There are always many vegetables, some vary from year to year; however, we seem to always have fresh green beans with new potatoes. We couldn't have Christmas without Praline Sweet Potato Casserole. People who don't even like sweet potatoes usually like this. It resembles a sweet potato pie without the crust.

On Christmas Eve morning all the dry ingredients for the dressing with the exception of the sage, salt, and pepper are assembled, covered, and set aside. The vegetables are sautéed, and the giblets and neck are boiled with the reserved broth. Everything is refrigerated until early Christmas morning when Mother and I usually assemble the dressing, with Dad giving lots of help in the "stuffing" department. Everyone usually brings one or two assigned dishes, and the women do all the last-minute preparation while the men sample, comment, and "visit."

It is a day you can count on pretty much being the same no matter where we are, or who joins us. It's definitely a comfort zone filled with many fond memories and cherished traditions.

*Susan Grohman*
*San Antonio, Texas*

# Christmas Eve Fiesta Luncheon

Our family has always celebrated Christmas Eve beginning with the noon meal and the menu listed below. Since my family, the Quinones, owns Jacala, the oldest originally owned Mexican restaurant in San Antonio, we have typical Mexican food for our Christmas Eve lunch. The recipe for Chicken Tamales is not included because they are made by hand and "by feel," so the measurements couldn't be given with any confidence. Also, the masa that is used for the tamales is also handmade, with no written recipe. My parents started Jacala in 1949, and we now have our third generation working there—as well as third and fourth generation customers.

*Lucille Hooker*
*San Antonio, Texas*

## Menu

Chicken Tamales

Chile Con Queso
*page 87*

Guacamole
*page 82*

Tortilla Chips

Polvorones
*page 203*

# Hanukkah Celebration

*anukkah,* an eight-day festival, commemorates the 2nd Century B.C.E. victory of the Jewish Maccabees over the Greek-Syrian forces that occupied and desecrated the Temple in Jerusalem.

*Hanukkah* is also called "the Festival of Lights," for when Judah Maccabee and his followers recaptured the Temple, they found insufficient oil for the Eternal Light. The small vial that was found was enough for only one day. Tradition says that, miraculously, the oil burned for eight days until additional oil could arrive.

Candles are lit every evening during the eight days of *Hanukkah.* A special eight-branch candle holder, called a *menorah,* is used. A special candle, which sits higher on the menorah, serves as the *shamash* (helper) and is used to light the candles. One candle is lit the first night, and an additional one is lit each night, until all eight are shining brightly. Blessings are offered, and a prayer is recited to celebrate the release of our people from oppression and the miracle of the oil that lasted for eight days. The evenings are spent in a joyous manner, with holiday songs and games.

The *Hanukkah* table usually includes special dishes. Different cultures have different traditions, and each family has its own, but most include certain deep-fried foods, to commemorate the "miracle of the oil." Ashkenazic Jews (usually of Eastern or Central European descent) eat *latkes* (potato pancakes) with applesauce and sour cream. Sephardic Jews (those whose ancestors lived in Spain) serve *bimuelos* (round doughnuts rolled in cinnamon honey). Israelis serve *sufganiyot* (jelly-filled doughnuts). Dairy dishes, such as kugels, blintzes and cheesecake, are also traditional for this festival.

## Menu

*Salmon Patties*

*Fresh Fruit Salad*

*Min's Noodle Kugel*
page 143

*Potato Latkes*
page 140

*from California Kosher*
*Women's League of*
*Adat Ari El Synagogue*
*North Hollywood, California*

# Christmas Eve in South Dakota

By Christmas Eve, winter usually has settled in for a good long stay in South Dakota. We look for a clean, soft snowfall on the 24th, followed by starry skies on Christmas night.

Our Christmas Eve has its share of such traditions as cookies cut from great-grandmother's tin cookie cutters and our voices harmonizing to "Silent Night." Each year is distinguished by the "first-timers"—the first time Andrew read the Christmas story and the first time we simultaneously dove into our presents instead of politely waiting for each to open the gifts one-at-a-time.

Christmas Eve dinner is full bloom of the season's anticipation and joy. If we don't always agree with each other throughout the year, we're unanimous around this table, set with the best dishes. The meal is a group effort, blended with German and Norwegian traditions and plenty of innovation. Mom (Marian Gunderson) makes Oyster Stew and Nina's Perfect Meatballs. My sister-in-law, Ann Schiefen, brings her Oatmeal Bread and the Norwegian potato flatbread, Lefse. I've mixed and rolled Grandmother Mae's Ginger Cookies for Andrew to transform into reindeer with silver bridles and Annicka to fashion into rainbow trout. After presents have been presented and received, my brother, John, would be surprised if the grand finale wasn't Lemon Pudding with the cookies.

It takes a whole year's tending and several lifetimes of memories to bring a family together for Christmas. And, don't forget the mashed potatoes.

*Mary Gunderson*
*St. Paul, Minnesota*

## Menu

**Oyster Stew**
*page 116*

**Nina's Perfect Meatballs**
*page 115*

**Browned carrots**

**Easy Lefse**
*page 102*

**Oatmeal-Molasses Rolls**
*page 103*

**Lemon Pudding**
*page 205*

**Grandmother's Ginger Cookies**
*page 186*

# Kwanzaa Celebration

**B**arbara Andrews from The National Civil Rights Museum in Memphis, Tennessee, shares some knowledge of the African-American holiday of Kwanzaa, which began in 1966 by Dr. Maulana Karenga. The celebration takes place from December 26 through January 1. It is a celebration of Africa and America, of the past and present and future. There are seven symbols of the celebration—the *mkeka* (a hand-woven mat), the *kinara* (candleholder for seven candles), *mishumaa saba* (candles), *mazao* (fruits and vegetables), *muhindi* (ears of corn), *kikombe cha umoja* (unity cup), and *zawadi* (gifts that are passed down through the generations or gifts that are created). Kwanzaa isn't a religious holiday or an alternative to Christmas, but rather a time to celebrate a harvest of family, friends, and culture. Seven principles are observed during this time—unity, self-determination, collective work and responsibility, cooperative economics, purpose, creativity, and faith. The sixth day of the celebration is used to show creativity—part of that being in the kitchen. The recipes shared here from the book *Kwanzaa Karamu* are Chapatis (a thin fried bread), Callaloo (a Caribbean soup made with callaloo greens or spinach), and Luku (an Ethiopian chicken dish).

## Menu

**Chapatis**
*page 105*

**Callaloo**
*page 118*

**Luku**
*page 119*

*Homemade Christmas*

# California Casual Holiday Supper

y husband, Kirk, and I often entertain friends over the holidays with a casual supper. The evening begins with a healthy smoked salmon appetizer that Kirk developed. Then while he cooks the steaks on the grill, I prepare a tossed salad of various greens and lots of chopped fresh vegetables. I also cook the Broccoli Rice casserole in the oven; the casserole can be combined before guests arrive and then baked while the steaks are sizzling. Broccoli Rice is a recipe from my mother, Audrey Corbello Coe, who lives in Lake Charles, Louisiana. I usually make her colorful Strawberry Delight for dessert, in addition to my moist Pumpkin Bread (after all, what would the holidays be like without pumpkin bread). After spending an enjoyable supper and evening with friends, I present them with a loaf of the Pumpkin Bread to take home.

**Candy Coe-Richardson**
**Huntington Beach, California**

## Menu

**Chef Rich's Smoked Salmon Appetizers**
*page 89*

**Grilled T-bone Steaks**

**Broccoli Rice**
*page 137*

**Tossed Green Salad**

**Strawberry Delight**
*page 202*

**Pumpkin Bread**
*page 203*

# Northwest Holiday Brunch

The Malm family consists of Joanne, me, and Cyrano (our dog). The Pacific Northwest has been my home for close to 30 years. Joanne comes from Hawaii. Since our family is small, for festive or holiday occasions we like to go all out in the preparation of a grand feast to which we invite our closest friends. The guest list usually tallies up to between 8 to 12 adults, and the occasional child or two. One need not live in the Pacific Northwest very long before the proximity to water and forest show up as primary sources for culinary inspiration and investigation. The Pacific Northwest is blessed with abundant seafood, which can be purchased fresh throughout the year. Salmon (fresh or smoked), Dungeness crab, clams, mussels, and oysters are the staples of Pacific Northwest cuisine. This menu and selected recipes represent a festive but casual holiday breakfast.

*Timothy Malm*
*Seattle, Washington*

## Menu

**Seafood Benedict with Hollandaise Sauce**
*page 129*

**Mixed Fruit with Honey Almond Sauce**
*page 139*

**Cranberry Scones with Citrus Butter**
*page 106*

**Coffee, Espresso, Lattes** *(Starbucks, Seattle's Best, Torrefazione)*

**Earl Grey, English Breakfast, Irish Breakfast Teas** *(loose leaf in teapots)*

# Party Time

## Christmas Music Dessert Buffet

**Theme:** After a performance of *The Messiah* or *A Christmas Carol* invite friends over for a dessert buffet. If your community doesn't have any live performances, rent a video of a favorite holiday movie, and finish the evening with the dessert buffet.

**Invitation Ideas:** Copy centers now carry beautiful holiday papers. Type the information for your party on a plain sheet of paper and have them copy it for you.

**Table Setting:** A simple vase of carnations or Christmas poinsettias will be enough. Everyone's focus will be on the dessert.

**Menu:** Find a balance in the menu; some guests may avoid sweets altogether, so offer a fruit and cheese tray as an alternative.

**Favors:** Send each guest home with a package of Christmas cookies.

### Menu

**Brandied Holiday Cakes**
*(page 209)*

**Bev's Chocolate Mousse**
*(page 207)*

**Fantasy Fudge**
*(page 50)*

**An assortment of Christmas cookies**

**Plum Pudding**
*(page 212)*

**Banana Bread**
*(page 105)*

# A Dickens Christmas

*An English countryside Christmas dinner*

🌀 **Theme:** For some reason, Christmas in England during the days of Dickens fascinates Americans. This holiday season, why don't you stage your own *A Dickens' Christmas*. Along with a meal reminiscent of Merry Olde England, you can include brief readings from *A Christmas Carol*, in particular the last page, where Scrooge has learned to keep Christmas better than any man alive!

🌀 **Invitation Ideas:** Tiny Tim Christmas cards can easily be converted into party invitations. Copy centers stock holiday paper. Select one that you like, and write your own invitation for the Copy center to create for you.

🌀 **Table Setting:** Incorporate your china. Search discount stores and factory outlets for elegant brass or silver napkin rings. Use a Christmas cloth or a simple white one. If you can't find napkin rings, use lengths of gold cording. Fresh evergreens and holly berries with candles make a fragrant centerpiece.

🌀 **Favors:** Set crackers at each place setting (shown at right). Fill with lumps of coal for those who've been bad and holiday mints for those who have been good. A copy of Charles Dickens' *A Christmas Carol* is also a wonderful gift.

## Menu

**Layered Holiday Salad**
*page 132*

**Creamy Peanut Soup**
*page 129*

**Pork Tenderloin**
*page 125*

**Roast Goose**
*page 126*

**Roasted onions and artichokes**

**Garlic mashed potatoes**
*page 141*

**Plum Pudding**
*page 212*

**Crème Brulée**

# Holiday Crackers

**MATERIALS:**
*Toilet paper rolls*
*Gift wrap or crepe paper*
*Gold stickers or decorative stickers*
*Ribbon, gold twine, raffia*
*Glitter or sequins (optional)*

*Though these will not go pop like commercial British crackers, they can be personalized and decorated to fit your style.*

🌀 Collect enough toilet paper rolls for each cracker you will need.

🌀 Fill each roll with small party favors, gifts, and candy.

🌀 Roll each roll in gift wrap or crepe paper.

🌀 Seal the paper together with a gold or festive sticker.

🌀 At each end of the roll, tie with ribbon, gold twine, or raffia.

🌀 Add glitter, sequins, or other designs to personalize your crackers.

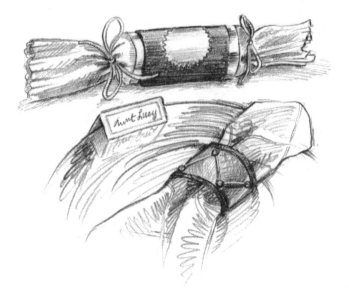

# A New Christmas Dinner Tradition

🌀 **Theme:** Rather than the traditional dinner, this year start a tradition of your own, especially if it's your turn to host the family.

🌀 **Invitation Ideas:** Send a handwritten note outlining the details of time, location, dress, what to bring.

🌀 **Table Setting:** Holiday topiaries and glass chimney centerpieces. Instructions on page 17.

🌀 **Favors:** Wine bottles decorated with mini wreaths (page 36) for the adults and jars of holiday goodies for the children.

## Menu

**Shrimp Cocktail**

**Boursin cheese**
*page 86*

**Caesar Salad**

**Stuffed Beef
Tenderloin**
*page 117*

**Rosemary Potatoes**
*page 140*

**Asparagus
Casserole**

**Cranberry relish**

**Mother's Whole
Wheat Rolls**
*page 107*

**Ambrosia**

**Mother's Coconut
Cake**
*page 210*

**Pecan Pie**

# Reindeer Party

🌀 **Theme:** A celebration of the reindeer who drive Santa's sleigh.

🌀 **Invitation Ideas:** Reindeer invitations from a party store or reindeer feet.

🌀 **Table Setting:** Wooden reindeers, paper and plastic, red-checked tablecloth or a Christmas cloth.

🌀 **Favors:** *Reindeer food:* In a holiday gift bag, put straw from a local garden center or feed store with uncut carrots for the children to place outside the front door on Christmas Eve. Place Reindeer Snack (page 88) in zip-top bags for the kids to take home, in addition to a Reindeer pin (page 35).

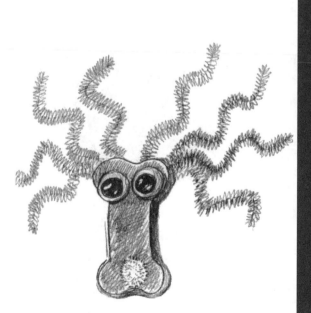

*Menu*

**Vegetables and crackers with North Pole dip (Ranch dressing)**

**Pimento, chicken salad, peanut butter sandwiches cut into a variety of shapes with Christmas ornaments**

**Chicken Noodle Soup**

**Sparkling Lemonade** *page 95*

**Fruit salad**

**Christmas cookies and ice cream**

*(All of the menu items can be picked up at the last minute prepared from your grocery or deli.)*

# Holiday Fiesta

🌀 **Theme:** Feliz Navidad—A Southwest Christmas

🌀 **Invitation Ideas:** Look for (or make your own) cowboy boot invitations.

🌀 **Table Setting:** Cactus decorated for Christmas in a clay pot with raffia ribbons. Napkins can be red and green bandannas.

🌀 **Favors:** Cowboy boot or cactus Christmas ornaments.

## Menu

**Margaritas and Sangria**
*page 95*

**Tortilla Chips and Salsa**
*page 88*

Chile con Queso dip
*page 87*

**Guacamole**
*page 82*

**Tortilla Soup**

**Chicken Enchilada Casserole**
*page 130*

**Spanish rice**

**Holiday Flan**

**Mexican Wedding Cookies**
*page 189*

**Cinnamon coffee**

*Homemade Christmas*

# New Year's Eve Gala

**⟳ Theme:** Glitz and Glamour, Black and White, Diamonds and Blue Jeans. You know your friends. Can you encourage them to dress up in black tie? Or is the most you can hope for blue jeans, boots, and maybe a tux jacket, à la Garth Brooks? Push your friends to the outer limits to welcome in the New Year. Start the party late, 9 or 10 p.m. to ensure that everyone is around when the clock strikes midnight.

**⟳ Invitation Ideas:** At a party store or stationery shop look for invitations with these possible designs:
*An hour glass or clock • Couples dancing under confetti • A baby*

**⟳ Table Setting:** Cover your table in an elegant but inexpensive piece of black satin or moiré fabric. Put small mirrors in several spots. Use only crystal, glass, and silver serving pieces. Place candles around the table. For an extra touch, save your white Christmas lights and circle your food plate trays with them to light up the table.

**⟳ Favors:** Hats and noisemakers

## Menu

*The time your party begins will dictate the menu. If you are beginning at 9 p.m., have heavy hors d'oeuvres including:*

Ham Biscuits
Beef Tenderloin
Crab Spread
Barbecued Chicken wings
page 76
Vegetable and cheese tray
Chips and dip
Stuffed mushrooms
page 78

*If the party starts later, have a few snacks and then serve a breakfast buffet after midnight. Include black-eyed peas to bring you and your friends luck and prosperity for the coming year.*

Sausage-Mushroom Breakfast
Casserole page 120
Hash browns
Black-eyed Peas page 136
Ham Biscuits
Fruit salad
Frozen Margarita Pie page 207
Brandied Holiday Cakes page 209
or Mother's Coconut Cake page 210

# *Twelfth Night Party*

We've always heard of the Twelve Days of Christmas, but rarely have we honored that tradition in the United States. From Christmas Day until January 6, the Epiphany, make up the 12 days of Christmas. The Epiphany marks the arrival of the Three Kings in Bethlehem, and it is claimed that on this occasion Christ was first revealed as divine to the Wise Men. In some countries, January 6 is the day that gifts are given to commemorate the Wise Men's gifts to the Christ Child.

**Theme:** January 6 is the day that the Wise Men presented gifts to the Christ Child. Since in our culture, we have given gifts on December 25, the Twelfth Night could be honored with a quiet celebration of family and friends, a closing of the holiday season.

**Invitation Ideas:** A manger scene with the Wise Men bearing gifts. Or a drawing of a gift box.

**Table Setting:** Gold stars symbolizing the star the Wise Men followed. Possibly a bowl of potpourri left over from your holiday decorations (see page 24).

**Favors:** Though the gift season is over, consider wrapping a small piece of wood or gift box in tapestry fabric; attach with a glue gun. Tie a bow using gold wired ribbon. Attach the following poem. Use at each place setting.

*This is a very special gift*
*That you can never see.*
*The reason it's so special is*
*It's filled with love from me.*

*Whenever you are lonely*
*Or if you are feeling blue.*
*Hold this gift close to your heart*
*And know I'm thinking of you.*

*Please don't ever unwrap it,*
*Always leave the ribbon tied.*
*Hold the box next to your heart*
*It's filled with love inside.*

## *Menu*

**Cheese Straws**
page 79

**White Bean Chili**
page 122

**or Winter Warming Stew**
page 111

**Colorful Christmas Coleslaw**
page 131

**South-of-the-Border Cornbread**
page 101

**Grandma's Chocolate Cake**
page 211

# Recipes for Festive Food

**From New England
Traditional to
California Casual**

*T*he holiday season is the time that everyone feels compelled to pull out all the stops. We expect our meals to be magical, delicious—and simple. We want to try new festive foods for our families and friends, and we want to be certain the new recipes won't flop!

The recipes in *Homemade Christmas* provide you delicious ideas to add to your holiday meals—from the Thanksgiving turkey to the Christmas ham.

Recipes from around the country have been included to add new ideas and twists to your holiday meals and celebrations. If a Southwest Christmas is what you have in mind, recipes for appetizers, casseroles, desserts, and beverages are included.

If you have always wanted to prepare an Olde English Christmas, try your hand at a Standing Rib Roast, Roast Goose, and Yorkshire Pudding.

The food should be festive, the beverages spirited, and best of all your company memorable.

# Appetizers

## Lobster and Green Goddess Dip

### 20 SERVINGS

1 clove garlic, minced

½ teaspoon salt

½ teaspoon dry mustard

1 teaspoon Worcestershire

3 tablespoons tarragon wine vinegar

2 tablespoons anchovy paste

3 tablespoons grated onion

⅓ cup chopped parsley

1 cup mayonnaise

½ cup sour cream

⅛ teaspoon pepper

4 (1-pound) frozen lobster tails

Combine first 11 ingredients for dressing. Cover and refrigerate overnight.

Cook the lobster tails the same day dip will be served. Drop tails in boiling salted water, and cook until bright red. Cool and cut into bite-size chunks. Serve on toothpicks with dip.

## Marinated Crab Claws

### 4 TO 6 SERVINGS

½ cup minced green onion

½ cup minced fresh parsley

1 stalk celery, minced

1 garlic clove, minced

½ cup olive oil

⅓ cup Italian dressing

2 tablespoons tarragon vinegar

¼ cup fresh lemon juice

½ cup water

Pinch of oregano

Worcestershire to taste

1 pound crab claws, steamed

Mix all ingredients except crab claws. Chill overnight. Add crab claws to marinade, and chill several hours. Serve cold.

## Barbecued Chicken Wings

### 10 TO 12 SERVINGS

3 pounds chicken wings

Salt and pepper to taste

½ cup honey

¼ cup soy sauce

4 tablespoons brown sugar

1 clove garlic, crushed

¼ cup ketchup

Cut up chicken wings, and remove tips. Arrange wings in foil-lined 13x9x2-inch pan. Sprinkle with salt and pepper. Combine honey, soy sauce, brown sugar, garlic, and ketchup. Pour over wings, and bake at 400° for 1 hour; turning and basting every 15 minutes.

# Oregon Salmon Balls

50 APPETIZERS

2 (7½-ounce) cans red salmon

1 (8-ounce) package cream cheese

1 tablespoon lemon juice

1 teaspoon horseradish

2 teaspoons grated onion

¼ teaspoon seasoned salt

6 tablespoons fresh chopped parsley

Combine all ingredients except parsley, and roll into small balls. Roll salmon balls in parsley.

# New England Clam Pinwheels

24 PINWHEELS

1 can minced clams

2 tablespoons onion

2 tablespoons butter, divided

1½ tablespoons flour

¼ teaspoon Worcestershire sauce

12 slices fresh white bread

Drain clams, reserving liquid; set aside. Sauté onion in 1 tablespoon butter, then blend in flour. Slowly add clam liquid; then add Worcestershire. Cook until mixture thickens. Add clams; cool.

Remove crusts from bread. Roll slices thin. Put a tablespoon of filling on each slice; roll up, and secure with a toothpick. Melt 1 tablespoon butter. Brush each roll with melted butter. Cut in half. Bake at 400° for 10 minutes. Serve hot.

# Stuffed Mushrooms

18 SERVINGS

**18 large mushrooms**

**1 (3-ounce) package cream cheese, softened**

**1 tablespoon milk**

**1 teaspoon Worcestershire sauce**

**¼ cup chopped water chestnuts**

**1 tablespoon minced green pepper**

**2 tablespoons minced green onions**

**2 tablespoons cooked, crumbled bacon**

Remove and finely chop stems of mushrooms. Beat cream cheese, milk, and Worcestershire sauce until light. Add chopped mushroom stems, water chestnuts, green pepper, onion, and bacon. Blend. Fill mushroom caps with mixture, and place on baking sheet. Bake at 350° for 15 minutes.

# Smoked Oyster Spread

1 CUP

**1 (3-ounce) package cream cheese**

**1 tablespoon mayonnaise**

**1 tablespoon sherry**

**1 tablespoon onion juice**

**1 tablespoon lemon juice**

**½ teaspoon curry powder**

**1 (4-ounce) can smoked oysters, drained and chopped**

**Minced chives**

Cream first 6 ingredients. Add oysters and chives. Chill.

# Cheese Straws

4½ DOZEN

**15 ounces extra sharp Cheddar cheese, grated**

**¾ cup butter**

**2 cups flour**

**½ teaspoon salt**

**1½ teaspoons baking powder**

**⅛ teaspoon hot sauce**

**1 to 2 teaspoons cayenne pepper**

Bring cheese and butter to room temperature; combine. Sift flour, salt, and baking powder together; add to cheese. Add hot sauce and cayenne; mix well. Roll out individual straws about 4 inches long and about the width of a pencil. Place on ungreased cookie sheet. Bake at 300° for 10 minutes. Lower oven to 225°, and bake until crisp.

# Barbecued Shrimp

12 TO 15 SERVINGS

**2 cloves garlic, crushed**

**½ cup oil**

**1 teaspoon salt**

**1 teaspoon ground pepper**

**3 tablespoons chili sauce**

**1 tablespoon Worcestershire sauce**

**3 tablespoons vinegar**

**2 tablespoons minced parsley**

**Dash hot sauce**

**3 pounds medium raw shrimp, shelled and deveined**

Combine first 9 ingredients in blender. Marinate shrimp in mixture for about 8 hours. Arrange shrimp on skewers, and broil over charcoal fire; turn frequently, and brush with marinade each time. Serve hot.

# Hot Crabmeat Spread

1 (8-ounce) package cream cheese

1 tablespoon milk

1 cup fresh flaked crabmeat

2 tablespoons finely chopped onion

¼ teaspoon seasoned salt

½ teaspoon horseradish

Dash pepper

⅓ cup toasted sliced almonds

Process first 7 ingredients in blender. Spoon into baking dish. Sprinkle with almonds. Bake at 375° for 15 minutes. Serve with crackers.

# Hot Spinach Balls

24 SERVINGS

2 (10-ounce) packages frozen chopped spinach

4 cups herb stuffing cubes

2 large onions, chopped

6 eggs, beaten

¾ cup melted butter

½ cup freshly grated Parmesan cheese

1 tablespoon garlic salt

½ teaspoon thyme

1 teaspoon pepper

1 teaspoon seasoned salt

Cook and drain spinach. Combine with remaining ingredients. Roll into balls, and chill overnight. Arrange on baking sheet, and bake at 350° for 20 minutes. Serve hot.

# Marinated Artichokes and Mushrooms

6 SERVINGS

**1 cup vinegar**

**½ cup oil**

**1 clove garlic, mashed**

**1 teaspoon salt**

**1 teaspoon ground pepper**

**½ teaspoon thyme**

**½ teaspoon oregano**

**1 tablespoon chopped parsley**

**1 Bermuda onion, thinly sliced**

**2 (7-ounce) cans artichokes, drained and sliced**

**2 pounds fresh mushrooms, sliced**

Combine vinegar, oil, garlic, salt, pepper, thyme, oregano, parsley, and onion; blend well. Add artichokes and mushrooms. Marinate overnight in refrigerator.

# Shrimp Quiches

24 SERVINGS

**3 tablespoons grated fresh Parmesan cheese**

**½ cup chopped, cooked shrimp**

**½ cup grated Swiss cheese**

**24 small tart shells**

**3 egg yolks**

**¾ cup light cream**

**Dash hot sauce**

**½ teaspoon salt**

Divide even amounts of Parmesan cheese, chopped shrimp, and Swiss cheese in bottoms of tart shells. Mix egg yolks, cream, hot sauce, and salt; fill tart shells with mixture. Bake at 325° for 15 minutes.

# Guacamole

### 6 TO 8 SERVINGS

**6 ripe avocados, mashed**

**Seasoned salt to taste**

**1 tomato, chopped**

**½ cup sour cream**

Mix all ingredients together well. Serve with tortilla chips.

# Southwest Hot Tamale Balls

### 150 MEATBALLS

**1 pound lean ground beef**

**1 pound pork sausage**

**1½ cups cornmeal**

**¾ cup tomato juice**

**¼ cup flour**

**3 cloves garlic, crushed**

**2 tablespoons chili powder, divided**

**4 teaspoons salt, divided**

**3 (14-ounce) cans tomatoes**

Combine first 6 ingredients with 1 tablespoon chili powder and 2 teaspoons salt; mix. Shape into small balls. Combine remaining chili powder, salt, and tomatoes in saucepan; bring to boil. Reduce heat and simmer. Drop meatballs into sauce. Simmer for 2 hours. Serve warm in chafing dish.

# Fiery Crescents

### 64 SERVINGS

1 pound ground beef

1 medium onion, finely chopped

1 teaspoon cumin

1 teaspoon oregano

1 teaspoon chili powder

¼ teaspoon cayenne pepper

2 tablespoons tomato paste

1 (8-ounce) container sour cream

1 cup grated Monterey Jack cheese

Dash of garlic salt

4 (8-ounce) cans crescent dinner rolls

1 egg, whisked with 1 tablespoon water

Brown beef and onion. Drain. Add next 8 ingredients and cook over medium heat. Remove from heat, and cool to room temperature. Separate rolls, and spread mixture on each. Roll into crescent shape, and brush with egg mixture. Bake at 375° for 10 to 15 minutes. Slice each roll in half, and serve hot.

*The stocking was always one of my favorite "presents" to explore on Christmas morning. I truly appreciated the stocking stuffers or little trinkets, candy, pecans, oranges, apples, and gum that were shoved inside. These things meant so much to me but cost so little. I'm sure my parents were mortified at times that I was more engrossed with a stocking full of $5 worth of junk than a $100 bicycle.*

*—Tracy Stand · Tucson, Az.*

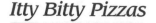

# Itty Bitty Pizzas

### 100 APPETIZERS

½ cup chopped bell pepper

½ cup chopped onion

1 to 2 tablespoons oil

½ pound sausage

½ pound ground beef

1 (8-ounce) can tomato sauce

1 pound mozzarella cheese, grated

1 pound sharp Cheddar cheese, grated

1 cup chopped ripe olives

½ cup chopped mushrooms

5 packages small party rolls (20 each)

Sauté pepper and onion in oil. Remove and set aside. Brown sausage and ground beef; drain. Combine pepper mixture, sausage mixture, and remaining ingredients, except rolls. Scoop out center of rolls; fill with pizza mix, and bake at 350° for 10 minutes. Serve hot.

# Chow Mein Nibbles

### 2½ CUPS

3 tablespoons butter

2 teaspoons soy sauce

Hot sauce to taste

1 (3-ounce) can chow mein noodles

¼ teaspoon celery salt

¼ teaspoon onion powder

Combine butter, soy sauce and hot sauce; drizzle over noodles. Toss lightly until noodles are well coated. Sprinkle noodles with celery salt and onion powder; toss. Bake at 275° for 12 to 15 minutes or until lightly browned and crisp.

# Sesame Chicken Bites

12 SERVINGS

**3 pounds boneless, skinless chicken breasts**

**1 cup mayonnaise**

**1 teaspoon dry mustard**

**2 teaspoons instant minced dried onion**

**1 cup Italian flavored breadcrumbs**

**½ cup sesame seeds**

*Honey Dip*

**2 cups mayonnaise**

**5 tablespoons honey**

Cut chicken into bite-size pieces; set aside. Combine mayonnaise, dry mustard, and onion; set aside. Combine crumbs and sesame seeds. Coat chicken pieces with mayonnaise mixture and then crumb mixture.

Arrange on baking sheet, and bake at 375° for 30 minutes. Whisk together the ingredients for the honey dip. Serve chicken hot or cold with honey dip.

# Cheese and Bacon Canapés

12 SERVINGS

**1 (3-ounce) package slivered almonds**

**1 tablespoon butter**

**½ pound sharp cheese, grated**

**8 slices bacon, cooked and crumbled**

**1 cup mayonnaise**

**1 small onion, grated**

**2 teaspoons Worcestershire sauce**

**1 loaf very thin white party bread**

Toast almonds in butter. Combine with remaining ingredients, except bread. Spread mixture on bread slices, and cut in four sections. Bake at 400° for 8 to 10 minutes.

# Boursin Cheese

### 16 SERVINGS

**2 (8-ounce) packages cream cheese**

**2 cloves garlic, minced**

**2 teaspoons caraway seed**

**2 teaspoons basil**

**2 teaspoons dill**

**2 teaspoons chives**

Blend all ingredients well. Take a piece of plastic wrap, and mold ingredients into a ball shape. To serve, place on a dish, and surround with crackers. Keep refrigerated.

*When Conrad Comeaux and I got married, I registered for Christmas china since we both had enough regular china to set up our household. Of course, I got a little of this and a little of that but not enough for a whole set. Each year, I invite both families over for Christmas dinner, and their present is to add a piece to the Christmas china. I now have 16 sets, and use them from Thanksgiving through New Year's.*

*— Jackie Lyle*     *Lafayette, La.*

# Meatballs in Cranberry Sauce

8 TO 10 SERVINGS

1½ pounds ground beef

½ pound ham, shredded

2½ cups packed soft breadcrumbs

2 tablespoons minced onion

¾ cup milk

2 eggs, slightly beaten

½ cup dry red wine

½ cup brown sugar

1 (16-ounce) can whole cranberry sauce

1 teaspoon ground cloves

1 tablespoon cornstarch

Combine ground beef, ham, breadcrumbs, onion, milk, and eggs. Shape into meatballs, and broil in broiler pan at 400° for 30 minutes. (Turn once during cooking.) Combine wine and brown sugar. Stir in cranberry sauce, cloves, and cornstarch.

Heat to warm. Place cooked meatballs in warm sauce, and serve in chafing dish.

# Chile Con Queso

6 TO 8 SERVINGS

1 (1-pound) loaf process cheese spread

1 (8-ounce) can Rotel tomatoes

Melt cheese on top of stove in double boiler. Add tomatoes to melted cheese. Serve hot with tortilla chips.

# Reindeer Snack

### ABOUT 9 CUPS

**3 cups popped unsalted popcorn**

**3 cups horn-shaped nacho cheese corn snacks**

**1 (4-ounce) can shoestring potatoes**

**2 cups pretzel sticks**

**⅓ cup butter or margarine, melted**

**½ teaspoon chili powder**

**1 clove garlic, finely chopped**

Mix popcorn, corn snacks, potatoes, and pretzels in large bowl. Mix remaining ingredients, and drizzle over popcorn mixture; toss to cover evenly. Spread on ungreased jellyroll pan.

Bake uncovered 15 minutes, stirring twice; cool. Store loosely covered at room temperature up to 2 weeks.

# Green Chile Salsa

### ABOUT 2 CUPS

**1 large tomato, chopped**

**1 small onion, chopped**

**3 green onions, finely chopped**

**2 tablespoons finely chopped pickled jalapeño pepper**

**2 tablespoons vinegar**

**1 tablespoon pickled jalapeño pepper juice, optional**

Combine first 4 ingredients in a small bowl. Stir in vinegar and pepper juice, if desired. Cover and chill until serving time.

# Chef Rich's Smoked Salmon Appetizers

### 8 TO 10 SERVINGS

**Zest of 2 oranges**

**Olive oil**

**1 baguette**

**½ pound goat cheese**

**2 tablespoons plain yogurt**

**1 teaspoon prepared horseradish**

**1 pound smoked salmon**

**Capers (for garnish)**

Finely grate orange zest. Place about ⅛-inch olive oil in medium saucepan. Add orange zest, and cook on high heat for about 1 minute. Do not burn. Remove from heat, and set aside.

Cut baguette into ½-inch slices; place on large cookie sheet. Brush orange mixture on slices, and place in oven on top rack. Broil until lightly toasted (about 30 to 60 seconds). Remove from oven.

Combine goat cheese, yogurt, and horseradish. Cut smoked salmon into 1-inch squares; place on baguette slices, and top with ½ to 1 teaspoon goat cheese mixture. Garnish with capers. Cover and chill.

*Chanukah time in our family was a special time for the family to get together and celebrate this holiday. We would gather at my aunt's home, where my grandparents lived, and have latkes, which are potato pancakes. The tradition at Chanukah was to give money called gelt; my grandfather would give each child a silver dollar from his tall chest of drawers in his bedroom. I will always remember this tradition at Chanukah time.*

*—Sheryl Heitin · Maitland, Fl.*

# Avocado Layered Dip

## 6 TO 8 SERVINGS

2 medium avocados, peeled and pitted

Dash of salt

Juice of ½ lemon

1 container frozen guacamole, thawed

1 cup sour cream

1 package taco seasoning mix

1 cup shredded Monterey Jack cheese

1 cup shredded Cheddar cheese

1 cup prepared salsa

Dash of hot pepper sauce

¼ cup chopped green onions

¼ cup chopped cilantro

¼ cup chopped ripe olives

Mash avocados with salt and lemon juice. Spread on bottom of serving dish. Spread guacamole over avocado. Combine sour cream and taco mix. Spread on top of guacamole. Top with cheeses. Pat down. Add chopped tomatoes evenly over all. Top with salsa. Sprinkle with hot sauce. Sprinkle green onions, cilantro, and olives over top. Serve with corn chips or tortillas.

# Beverages

## Christmas Mulled Cider

4 (8-OUNCE) SERVINGS

**4 cups apple cider**

**1 teaspoon cinnamon**

**4 cloves**

**¼ teaspoon orange extract**

**Cinnamon sticks**

Heat cider, cinnamon, cloves, and orange extract until warm. Pour into mugs, and serve with cinnamon sticks.

## Santa's Spritzer

9 (6-OUNCE) SERVINGS

**4 cups cranberry juice cocktail**

**1 cup orange juice**

**2 cups ginger ale or diet ginger ale**

Mix cranberry juice cocktail, orange juice, and soda together. Garnish with orange slices.

## Frosty Peppermint Shake

4 SERVINGS

**3 cups milk**

**¼ cup crushed candy canes**

**1 cup vanilla frozen yogurt**

**1 tablespoon sugar**

**½ teaspoon peppermint flavoring**

Combine all ingredients in blender, and mix at medium speed until smooth. Serve immediately.

## Sunshine Party Punch

26 (6-OUNCE) SERVINGS

**1 quart orange juice**

**1 quart pineapple juice**

**1 quart apple juice**

**1 quart ginger ale**

**1 quart seltzer water**

**Orange rings (optional)**

**Pineapple chunks (optional)**

Mix juices, soda, and seltzer together in punch bowl. Garnish with orange rings and pineapple chunks, if desired. Refrigerate before serving.

## Tangy Green Sparkling Cream

8 (8-OUNCE) SERVINGS

**2 cups lime sherbet**

**1 quart lemon-lime soda**

**2 cups seltzer water**

**Lime slices (optional)**

Soften sherbet to room temperature. Place in punch bowl, and mix with soda and seltzer water. Garnish with lime slices, if desired.

*Homemade Christmas*

# Raspberry Punch

### 13 (6-OUNCE) SERVINGS

**1 quart raspberry juice cocktail**

**1 quart cranberry juice cocktail**

**2 cups orange juice**

**Orange slices (optional)**

**Raspberries (optional)**

Mix first 3 ingredients together. Garnish with orange slices and raspberries, if desired. Refrigerate before serving.

# Milk Punch

### 1 GALLON

*This drink is quite popular in old New Orleans restaurants and is a favorite during the winter holiday season. It is a soothing drink after a night of partying.*

**1 (⅘-quart) bottle of bourbon or brandy**

**3 quarts half-and-half**

**4 tablespoons vanilla extract**

**Simple Syrup**

**Grated nutmeg**

Combine the bourbon, half-and-half, and vanilla in a 1-gallon container. Add the Simple Syrup to attain desired sweetness. Chill thoroughly. Serve in a chilled glass (not over ice), and sprinkle with nutmeg.

# Simple Syrup

**1 cup water**

**1 cup sugar**

Combine sugar and water in a small saucepan; boil until sugar dissolves and liquid becomes slightly thick. Cool completely before using.

# Bloody Marys

### 4 DRINKS

*This is a real eye-opener when spiced with Louisiana's own
Tabasco.*

**4 cups thick tomato juice**

**1 teaspoon salt**

**1 teaspoon black pepper**

**½ teaspoon celery salt**

**1 tablespoon Worcestershire sauce**

**8 to 10 dashes Tabasco**

**2 teaspoons fresh lime juice**

**4 to 5 jiggers vodka**

**Lime wedges for garnish**

In a large pitcher, combine all ingredients except lime wedges, and
chill for at least 1 hour. Stir again before serving. Pour into tall
glasses over chipped ice; garnish with lime.

I can remember Christmases when I was young
when Daddy always placed a large box of
Whitman's Sampler chocolates under the tree.
This was a special treat because we didn't
eat much candy throughout the year. I
continue the tradition each year for my
family, but the box of chocolates I place
under the tree doesn't seem as large.

—Carole Sharpe · Memphis, Tn.

*Homemade Christmas*

# Sparkling Lemonade

### 9½ CUPS

**1 (12-ounce) can frozen lemonade concentrate, thawed**

**2 cups pineapple juice**

**2 (23-ounce) bottles sparkling mineral water**

Combine all ingredients, stirring well. Serve over ice.


# Frozen Margaritas

### 6 TO 8 (5-OUNCE) SERVINGS

**1 (6-ounce) can frozen limeade**

**9 ounces tequila**

**2 ounces triple sec**

**⅛ lime, diced**

**Coarse salt**

Put first 4 ingredients in blender. Fill with ice, and blend until smooth. Rub edges of glasses with lime, and dip in coarse salt. Pour margaritas into glasses, and serve


# Sangria

### ABOUT 2 QUARTS

**1 (750 ml) bottle Burgundy**

**1 (10-ounce) bottle club soda**

**½ cup brandy**

**1½ ounces Cointreau**

**3 tablespoons sugar**

**Juice of 2 oranges, 1 lemon, and 1 lime**

Mix first 6 ingredients in a glass pitcher. Garnish with cherries and fruit slices. Refrigerate for at least 8 hours. Serve in tall glasses over ice.

# Breads

## Chocolate Lovers' Muffins

### 12 MUFFINS

½ **stick butter, softened**

1 **cup sugar**

1 **egg**

1 **cup flour**

1 **teaspoon baking powder**

**Dash salt**

⅓ **cup water**

1 ½ **squares bitter chocolate, melted**

1 **teaspoon vanilla**

Cream butter and sugar until light and fluffy. Add one egg, and beat well. Sift flour, baking powder, and salt together. Mix dry ingredients into creamed mixture alternately with water. (Start with flour mixture). Add melted bitter chocolate and 1 teaspoon vanilla. Stir. Fill greased muffin tins two-thirds full. Bake at 400° for 12 minutes.

# Apple Bread

### 1 LOAF

1 ½ cups flour

2 tablespoons baking powder

½ teaspoon baking soda

1 teaspoon salt

1 teaspoon cinnamon

¼ teaspoon nutmeg

⅛ teaspoon allspice

½ cup wheat germ

1 cup wheat flakes

1 cup chopped walnuts

1 cup unpeeled, chopped red apple

1 egg, slightly beaten

¾ cup packed brown sugar

1 ½ cups buttermilk

2 tablespoons vegetable oil

Sift together flour, baking powder, and next 5 ingredients. Stir in wheat germ, wheat flakes, walnuts, and apple. Stir in remaining 4 ingredients, just enough to mix. Turn into buttered 9x5x3-inch pan. Bake at 350° for 1 hour.

In Michigan City, Mississippi, my parents, Lamar and Linda Miller, always got the whole family together for Christmas breakfast before opening presents. That included children, their spouses, and grandchildren. Breakfast consists of homemade biscuits and Chocolate Gravy (see Page 206). What a way to start the day.

— Sandy Hensley · Walls, Ms.

# Lemon Loaves

### 3 LOAVES

½ pound butter

2½ cups sugar, divided

4 eggs

2 lemons, squeezed and rind grated

3 cups flour

2 teaspoons baking powder

1 teaspoon salt

1 cup milk

Cream cheese, softened

Cream butter and 2 cups sugar together; add eggs one at a time, beating after each addition. Add lemon rind. Add sifted dry ingredients alternately with milk. Turn into three 9x5x3-inch loaf pans; bake at 350° for 45 to 60 minutes. Place on wire racks covered with waxed paper. Combine remaining sugar with juice of lemons; drizzle over loaves, and cool. Serve with cream cheese.

*My mother from North Louisiana typically prepares her yummy oyster-cornbread dressing and giblet gravy for the holiday feast. My mother-in-law does a delicious Cajun-style turkey. It has little slits all over that are stuffed with garlic and Cajun seasonings. She serves it with rice dressing (the Cajun kind with liver, onion, garlic and roux). I often make cranberry-walnut conserve (see Page 39). Another wonderful Cajun recipe, Crawfish Cornbread Dressing, from Hattie M. Andrews can be found on page 140.*

*—Sandra Day · Lafayette, La.*

# Sour Cream Loaf

### 2 LOAVES

1 cup sour cream

1 package egg custard mix

2 cups flour

2½ teaspoons baking powder

½ teaspoon baking soda

1 teaspoon salt

½ cup milk

Cinnamon sugar

Combine sour cream and custard mix; beat until smooth. Add next 5 ingredients; mix thoroughly. Pour into two greased small loaf pans. Sprinkle cinnamon sugar on top, and bake at 375° for 20 to 25 minutes.

# Squash Blossom Muffins

### 2 DOZEN

1 cup milk

⅔ cup cooked yellow squash

¼ cup sugar

1 egg, beaten

2¾ cups flour

3 teaspoons baking powder

1 teaspoon salt

1 tablespoon melted butter

Add milk to squash; then add sugar and eggs, and set aside. Sift together flour, baking powder, and salt. Add to first mixture; then add butter. Beat thoroughly. Spoon into greased muffin pans. Bake at 375° for 25 minutes.

# Zucchini Bread

### 2 LOAVES

3 eggs

2 cups sugar

1 cup oil

2 ounces unsweetened chocolate

1 teaspoon vanilla

2 cups grated zucchini

3 cups flour

1 teaspoon cinnamon

1 teaspoon salt

1/4 teaspoon baking powder

1 teaspoon baking soda

1 cup chopped nuts

Cream cheese, softened

Grated orange rind

Beat eggs until lemon colored. Beat in sugar and oil. Melt chocolate, and stir into egg mixture with vanilla and zucchini. Sift dry ingredients together, and stir into zucchini mixture. Add nuts. Place in two greased 9x5x3-inch loaf pans. Bake at 350° for 50 to 60 minutes. Cool in pans 15 minutes, and turn out of racks to cool. Spread tops with cream cheese, and sprinkle with orange rind.

# Herbed Pita Bread

### 4 SERVINGS

1 (14-ounce) package pita bread

1/4 pound butter

1 teaspoon dried parsley flakes

1 teaspoon garlic powder

1 teaspoon lemon juice

Slice each pocket bread in 4 pieces. Combine all other ingredients; mix well. Spread each quarter slice lightly. Arrange on cookie sheet, and bake at 275° for 30 minutes.

# South-of-the-Border Cornbread

### 8 TO 10 SERVINGS

1 cup cornmeal

1 cup milk

3 eggs

3 jalapeño peppers, seeded and chopped

½ cup chopped onion

1 teaspoon garlic powder

1½ cups grated Cheddar cheese

½ teaspoon baking soda

½ teaspoon salt

½ teaspoon sugar

1 cup whole kernel corn, drained

1 (2-ounce) can chopped pimiento, drained

⅓ cup oil

Combine all ingredients; stir until thoroughly blended. Cook in well-greased heavy skillet at 350° for 45 minutes.

*Every year, for as long as I can remember, my mom, Kathleen Lentz, has made gift baskets for the elderly, sick, shut-ins, and neighbors. The baskets consist of homemade candy and cookies, a homemade arts and crafts item, fruit, and a store-bought gift (frame, kitchen magnet etc.). She adorns the baskets with ribbons and colorful Christmas decorations and delivers them to those who need a bit of cheer during the holiday season.*

*—Maureen Fortune · Arkabutla, Ms.*

# Easy Lefse

### ABOUT 5½ DOZEN

*Lefse is a Norwegian flatbread served either as a treat or with the meal.*

**9 cups boiling water**
**1½ cups butter or margarine**
**9 cups instant potato flakes**
**3 cups powdered milk**
**⅓ cup granulated sugar**
**5 teaspoons salt**
**4½ cups all-purpose flour, divided**

In a large pot, combine water and butter, and heat until butter melts. In a large bowl, combine potato flakes, milk, sugar, and salt. Stir mixture into hot water and butter, mixing well. Cover and refrigerate overnight.

Remove one-third batch at a time from refrigerator, and stir in 1½ cups flour to each batch. Form into 1¼-inch balls. Cover remaining dough with plastic wrap. On floured surface, roll each ball into a thin, 8- to 9-inch round sheet. Roll sheet around rolling pin, and unroll on hot, ungreased griddle or 14-inch frying pan. Fry until lefse is light-colored and dry on top. Turn lefse, and fry on other side a minute or two. Cool on wire racks, and stack cooled lefse to store. Repeat with remaining dough.

To serve, spread with softened butter, and sprinkle with sugar. Roll to eat.

# Oatmeal-Molasses Rolls

### 2 DOZEN ROLLS OR 2 LOAVES BREAD

**2 cups boiling water**

**1 cup quick or old-fashioned oatmeal**

**½ cup light mild molasses**

**1 ½ teaspoons salt**

**1 tablespoon melted butter**

**1 package active dry yeast**

**4 ½ to 5 cups all-purpose flour**

In a large bowl, pour boiling water over oatmeal. Add molasses, salt, and butter. Cool to 110°, and add yeast. Allow to stand for 5 to 10 minutes. Stir in flour, 1 cup at a time until dough is easy to handle. Knead on floured board for about 10 minutes or until dough is smooth and elastic. Cover and let rise until doubled in warm place for about an hour.

Punch dough down, and form into buns or loaves. Place on greased baking sheet or in greased 9x5x3-inch loaf. Cover and let rise in warm place 45 minutes to 1 hour.

Bake at 375° for 15 to 20 minutes for rolls, about 40 minutes for loaves or until tops are golden and rolls or loaves sound hollow when tapped. Cool on wire racks.

# Capt'n Allen's Anadama Bread

### 2 LOAVES

**1¾ cups water, divided**

**1 teaspoon salt**

**⅓ cup cornmeal**

**⅓ cup molasses**

**1½ teaspoons margarine**

**1 package active yeast**

**4 to 4½ cups flour**

Place 1½ cups water and salt in a saucepan; bring to a boil. Stir in cornmeal; return water to boiling point, stirring constantly. Pour mixture into a large bowl. Stir in molasses and margarine. Cool to lukewarm, about 115°. Dissolve yeast in ¼ cup warm water. Add to cornmeal mixture, and mix well. Add flour, about 1 cup at a time; use hands when mixture gets too stiff to stir. Turn out onto board, and knead well (at least 10 minutes). Place in a greased bowl, cover with a damp cloth, and let rise until double in bulk (about 1½ hours). Remove to the board, punch down, and shape into two loaves. Put in greased pan, and let rise until double in bulk, about 1 hour. Bake at 375° for 40 to 45 minutes.

# Banana Bread

### 1 LOAF

**1 cup sugar**

**2 eggs**

**½ cup oil**

**1¼ cups all-purpose flour**

**1 teaspoon baking soda**

**½ teaspoon salt**

**½ cup chopped pecans**

**3 small bananas, mashed**

Mix all ingredients together. Pour into greased loaf pan. Bake for 1 hour at 325° or until toothpick comes out clean when placed in center of loaf.

# Chapatis

### 6 SERVINGS

**⅓ teaspoon salt**

**3 cups unbleached all-purpose flour, divided**

**¾ cup plus 1 to 3 tablespoons vegetable oil**

**¾ to 1 cup water**

In a large bowl, mix salt and 2½ cups flour. Add ¾ cup oil, and mix well. Add water a little at a time, stirring after each addition, until dough is soft. Knead dough in bowl for 5 to 10 minutes. Sprinkle about ¼ cup flour on a flat surface. Take a 2-inch ball of dough, and roll into a ⅛-inch-thick circle. Repeat with remaining dough.

Heat 1 tablespoon oil over medium-high heat for 1 minute. Fry 3 to 5 minutes per side or until brown. Remove from pan, and let drain on paper towels. Fry remaining chapatis, adding more oil if necessary. Serve immediately or place in a covered container until ready to serve.

# Cranberry Scones with Citrus Butter

**12 TO 16 SCONES**

**2 ½ cups flour, divided**

**½ cup sugar**

**1 ½ tablespoons baking powder**

**½ cup chilled unsalted butter**

**½ cup dried cranberries or dried currants**

**½ cup heavy cream**

**3 eggs**

**1 tablespoon cold water**

**Citrus Butter**

In a large bowl, mix 2 cups flour with sugar and baking powder. Cut butter into small cubes. Add it to the flour mix. Cut in with a pastry cutter until mixture resembles coarse meal. Add dried cranberries; blend.

Make a well in the center of the mixture. Add the heavy cream and 2 eggs. Fold ingredients together. Do not overmix. Dough will be soft. Turn out onto floured board. Knead while adding the reserved flour. Add flour until dough is just stiff enough to be rolled out.

Roll dough into four 1-inch-thick circles. Cut into wedges. Place on a well-greased cookie sheet. Mix the remaining egg with the water. Brush eggwash over scones. Bake at 350° for 15 minutes or until golden brown.

## Citrus Butter

**½ cup butter**

**1 tablespoon orange, lemon, or lime juice**

**1 tablespoon honey**

**1 teaspoon zest of orange**

Place ingredients in a small bowl; blend thoroughly. Serve with warm scones. Preserves are a natural with the scones.

# Mother's Whole Wheat Rolls

1 ½ TO 2 DOZEN ROLLS

**1 package dry yeast**

**1 cup lukewarm water**

**½ cup oil**

**⅓ cup sugar**

**1 egg, beaten**

**1 teaspoon salt**

**1 teaspoon baking powder**

**1 ½ cups whole wheat flour**

**1 ½ cups self-rising white flour, sifted**

Dissolve yeast in lukewarm water. Add oil, sugar, egg, salt, baking powder, and whole wheat flour. Beat well. Add white flour. Stir in well. Cover and let rise 2 hours or more.

Punch dough down, and turn out on floured board. Knead just until smooth. Roll out to make rolls. Place rolls on greased baking sheet, and brush tops with melted butter. Let rise 1 to 1½ hours. Bake at 400° for 12 to 15 minutes.

# Entrées

## Delicious Holiday Ham

### 18 TO 20 SERVINGS

**1 (10- to 12-pound) country ham**
**2 (12-ounce) cans cola**
**Honey mustard**
**Whole cloves**
**Brown sugar**

Soak ham in water for 4 hours. Place ham in a roaster, fat side down. Pour cola over ham. Cover top of ham with aluminum foil.

Place ham in a cold oven, and set temperature at 500°. Bake ham for 20 minutes. Turn oven off. Leave ham in oven for 2 hours; do not open oven door. After 2 hours, set oven at 500° again, and bake ham for 15 minutes. Leave ham another 3 to 8 hours.

Skin ham, leaving a very thin layer of fat. Coat ham with honey mustard and brown sugar. Dot with cloves. Brown under broiler. Slice, and serve.

# Roast Turkey

### 10 TO 12 SERVINGS

**1 (8- to 10-pound) turkey**
**1 stick butter, melted**
**1 tablespoon Worcestershire sauce**
**Greek seasoning (Cavender's, if possible)**

Remove parts from inside of turkey and from the neck; save for gravy or stuffing if desired. Clean turkey well. Mix butter and Worcestershire, and brush on turkey inside and out. Sprinkle inside and out with Greek seasoning.

Place turkey in large roasting pan. Bake at 350° for 3 to 4 hours. Use a meat thermometer for accuracy to test for doneness. Thermometer should be placed in the inner thigh and should reach 180° to 185° for doneness.

When done, remove from oven, let turkey stand for 10 or 15 minutes, and move to serving plate for carving.

# Rich Red Chili

### 6 SERVINGS

**½ pound ground turkey breast**
**½ pound ground beef**
**½ cup chopped onion**
**1 teaspoon chili powder**
**1 teaspoon cumin**
**¼ teaspoon cayenne pepper**
**1 (28-ounce) can diced tomatoes**
**1 (15-ounce) can red kidney beans**

Brown turkey and beef in nonstick Dutch oven with onion and spices. Add tomatoes and kidney beans, including canned liquid. Cover, simmer over low heat until meat is completely cooked and vegetables thoroughly warmed.

# Marinated Turkey Breast

### 4 SERVINGS

**1 pound turkey breast slices**

**¼ cup lemon juice**

**2 tablespoons red wine vinegar**

**2 teaspoons black pepper**

**1 clove minced garlic**

**1 tablespoon minced chives**

Pierce turkey breast slices, and place in shallow dish. Combine remaining ingredients, and pour over turkey. Marinate for 1 to 2 hours. Turkey breasts can be prepared by broiling, baking, or sautéing.

# Seasoned Chicken Breast Strips

### 4 TO 6 SERVINGS

**¼ cup lemon juice**

**¼ cup water**

**1 tablespoon vegetable oil**

**1 teaspoon vinegar**

**1 teaspoon black pepper**

**½ teaspoon onion powder**

**½ teaspoon garlic powder**

**3 boneless chicken breasts, cut into strips**

Combine liquids and seasonings; mix well. Pour over chicken, allow to marinate in refrigerator for 1 to 2 hours. Seasoned chicken breast strips can be steamed or stir-fried with mixed vegetables.

## Salmon Patties

2 TO 3 SERVINGS

1 (6-ounce) can water-packed salmon

1 egg

2 tablespoons seafood seasoned breadcrumbs

1 tablespoon finely chopped onion

1 teaspoon salt-free lemon/pepper seasoning

Combine all ingredients; mix well. Shape salmon mixture into patties. Sauté in oil in frying pan, or broil on rack 2 to 3 inches from heat until well browned on both sides.

## Winter Warming Stew

8 SERVINGS

1 (10½-ounce) can chicken broth

2 cups frozen sliced carrots

2 cups frozen green beans

1 (28-ounce) can crushed tomatoes

½ teaspoon thyme

1 teaspoon pepper

1 bay leaf

16 ounces shell pasta, cooked and drained

Combine all ingredients except pasta in large pot over medium heat, and cook until vegetables are tender. Reduce heat, add pasta, and continue cooking until thoroughly heated.

# Santa's Simmering Pork Chops

### 4 SERVINGS

**½ teaspoon vegetable oil**

**1 pound boneless sirloin pork chops**

**½ cup sliced onion**

**1 cup apple juice**

Heat oil in nonstick pan. Add pork chops and onion, and cook until chops are brown on both sides. Add apple juice, cover, reduce heat, and simmer until chops are thoroughly cooked.

# Glazed Ham

### ABOUT 10 TO 12 SERVINGS

*You can remove the skin from the ham, but if you leave it on, it provides delightful tidbits to munch on once the ham is cooked.*

**1 (8-pound) ham shank**

**Whole cloves**

**1 cup port wine, divided**

**1 tablespoon dry mustard**

**1 ½ tablespoons dark brown sugar**

**½ cup ginger ale**

Score the skin and/or fat by making long vertical or horizontal cuts. Bake ham at 300° for 30 minutes. Remove the ham from the oven, and place whole cloves in the center of each scored section. Return the ham to the oven for another 30 minutes, basting with ½ cup of the port wine.

Mix the dry mustard, brown sugar, and remaining port together in a small bowl. Remove the ham from the oven, and spread the mustard mixture over the top. Pour the ginger ale into the bottom of the pan.

Raise the heat to 450°, and return the ham to the oven. Baste every 10 to 15 minutes with pan juices. Continue to bake for about 1 hour. Loosely cover the ham with foil for this last hour of cooking. If you need more basting liquid, add more port and ginger ale.

# Scrambled Egg Casserole

### 8 TO 10 SERVINGS

1 cup cubed ham or Canadian bacon

¼ cup chopped green onions

3 tablespoons butter, melted

1 dozen eggs, beaten

1 (4-ounce) can mushrooms, drained

Cheese Sauce

2¼ cups breadcrumbs

½ cup butter, melted

⅛ teaspoon paprika

Sauté ham and green onions in 3 tablespoons of butter in large skillet until onions are tender. Add eggs and cook, stirring to form large, soft curds. When eggs are set, stir in mushrooms and Cheese Sauce. Spoon eggs into a greased 13x9x2-inch baking pan.

Combine ½ cup melted butter with the breadcrumbs. Spread evenly over egg mixture. Sprinkle with paprika. Cover and chill overnight. Uncover and bake at 350° for 30 minutes.

# Cheese Sauce

1 cup grated Cheddar cheese

2 tablespoons butter

2½ tablespoons flour

2 cups milk

½ teaspoon salt

⅛ teaspoon pepper

Mix all ingredients in saucepan; heat until cheese melts. Keep warm until ready to use.

# Roast Beef and Yorkshire Pudding

### 6 SERVINGS

**1 (4-pound) standing rib roast**

**Seasonings to taste**

Keep roast in refrigerator until ready to cook. Preheat oven to 350°. Place roast on rack in baking pan, fat side up. Season to taste. Do not cover or baste. Cook about 20 minutes per pound, or until internal temperature reaches 140° (for rare) in the center of the roast. Serve with Yorkshire Pudding.

## Yorkshire Pudding

**1 cup sifted flour**

**2 large eggs**

**½ teaspoon salt**

**1 cup milk**

**Meat drippings**

Beat flour, eggs, salt, and milk until smooth. Let stand at room temperature for 30 minutes. In a 12x7½x2-inch baking dish, heat the meat drippings from the roast until sizzling. Stir in the batter. Bake in a 425° oven for 35 to 45 minutes (check after 30 minutes), or until golden brown. Serve immediately.

## Quick Bouillabaisse

### 12 SERVINGS

**3 (10¾-ounce) cans cream of shrimp soup**

**1 pound frozen lobster, broken into bite-size bits**

**2 (4⅓-ounce) cans shrimp, drained and washed**

**3 tablespoons butter**

**2 tablespoons chopped green onion**

**1 tablespoon chopped parsley**

Place all ingredients in large double boiler. Cook over medium heat for 20 to 30 minutes. Stir occasionally to blend ingredients well.

*Homemade Christmas*

# Nina's Perfect Meat Balls

### ABOUT 8 SERVINGS

1½ **pounds ground beef**

½ **pound ground pork**

¼ **cup finely chopped onion**

2 **tablespoons finely chopped celery**

2 **teaspoons salt**

½ **teaspoon poultry seasoning**

¼ **teaspoon pepper**

½ **cup milk**

2 **eggs**

¼ **teaspoon dry mustard**

1 **teaspoon Worcestershire sauce**

4 **slices dry bread, cubed**

In a large bowl, combine meats well. Stir in onion, celery, and seasonings. In a small bowl, combine milk, eggs, dry mustard, and Worcestershire. Soak bread for several minutes; then beat well, and combine with meat mixture. Chill 1 hour.

Form into 1½-to 2-inch balls. Place in a 13x9x2-inch baking pan. Bake at 400° for about 25 minutes until browned and cooked through. Serve with hot mashed potatoes.

# Oyster Stew

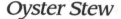

**ABOUT 8 SERVINGS**

**4 cups water**

**1 ⅓ cups nonfat milk**

**1 (12-ounce) can evaporated milk**

**1 tablespoon butter or margarine**

**1 cup fresh or canned oysters with liquid**

**Salt, pepper, and Worcestershire sauce to taste**

In soup kettle, bring water to boiling. Reduce heat to simmer. Whisk in milks.

In another pan, melt butter. Add oysters, and cook over medium heat until edges of oysters curl and color is dull gray. (Don't overcook.) Add oysters to stewed milk. Simmer 5 to 10 minutes, stirring often to reduce sticking to bottom of pan. Season to taste.

To serve, ladle into warm bowls.

*It never failed that every year we would lose at least one ornament from our Christmas decorations because the tree stood on linoleum floors. One year, the entire holiday season passed with no broken ornaments. Since it seemed to be a tradition, my brother and I argued over who would break that year's decoration. The argument heated up but ended quickly as we heard a smash. Mother decided to do the honors (mostly to stop the fighting), making it the most memorable year of the broken ornaments.*

*—David Cullen · Kansas City, Mo.*

*Homemade Christmas*

# Stuffed Tenderloin

### 4 SERVINGS

**2 green peppers**

**2 red peppers**

**2 onions**

**2 tablespoons minced garlic**

**2 tablespoons of fresh rosemary, thyme, marjoram**

**¼ cup olive oil**

**1 (2-pound) beef or pork tenderloin**

**1 cup red wine**

**½ cup Worcestershire sauce**

**2 tablespoons crushed garlic**

**2 tablespoons Cavender's seasoning**

Thinly slice the peppers and onions. Sauté onion, pepper, garlic, and herbs in ¼ cup olive oil until soft. Cool.

Slice tenderloin in the middle but do not sever completely. In the center, place the pepper and onion mixture. Roll tenderloin together, and tie both ends and center with string. Marinate the tenderloin two hours in red wine, Worcestershire, and crushed garlic.

Before cooking, rub the tenderloin with Cavender's seasoning. Bake for 20 to 30 minutes on 400°. Check to see if the meat is done (serve pink). Slice and serve.

# Callaloo

### 4 TO 6 SERVINGS

4 tablespoons butter or margarine
1 small onion, chopped
1 clove garlic, peeled and chopped
3 cups chicken broth
½ cup unsweetened coconut milk
1 medium potato, peeled and chopped
1 teaspoon salt
1 ½ teaspoons black pepper
¾ pound fresh spinach, cleaned and chopped
½ pound cooked crabmeat
Paprika

In a large kettle, melt butter over medium-high heat. Add onion and garlic, and sauté for about 5 minutes or until onion is translucent. Add chicken broth, coconut milk, potato, salt, and pepper to kettle; stir well. Boil over high heat. Reduce heat to low and cover, leaving cover slightly ajar. Simmer for 15 minutes.

Add spinach and simmer, uncovered, for 10 minutes or until spinach is tender. Add crabmeat, and stir well. Cook for another 5 minutes or until heated through. Sprinkle with paprika, and serve hot.

# Luku

## 6 SERVINGS

**8 hard-boiled eggs, peeled**

**¾ cup vegetable oil, divided**

**5 to 6 cups chopped onion**

**¼ cup tomato paste**

**½ cup water**

**2 teaspoons salt**

**¾ teaspoon black pepper**

**1¼ tablespoons garlic, peeled and minced**

**2 teaspoons paprika**

**¼ teaspoon ground cumin (optional)**

**8 pieces chicken**

With a sharp knife, make 4 to 5 shallow cuts on both sides of each egg; set aside. Heat 2 tablespoons oil over medium-high heat for 1 minute. Add onion, and sauté for 8 to 10 minutes or until onion starts to turn brown. Reduce heat to medium, and add tomato paste and water; stir well. Cook for 10 minutes; then add remaining oil. Cook for 5 minutes more. Add salt, pepper, garlic, paprika, cumin, and chicken. Reduce heat to low and simmer, uncovered, for about 30 minutes. Add eggs, cover, and cook for 10 minutes or until chicken is tender.

# Sausage-Mushroom Breakfast Casserole

### 8 SERVINGS

**2¼ cups seasoned croutons**

**1 pound pork sausage, cooked, drained and crumbled**

**4 eggs, beaten**

**2¼ cups milk**

**1 (10¾-ounce) can cream of mushroom soup (undiluted)**

**1 (4-ounce) can sliced mushrooms, drained**

**¾ teaspoon dry mustard**

**2 cups shredded Cheddar cheese**

Spread croutons in a lightly greased 13x9x2-inch baking dish; set aside. Sprinkle sausage over croutons. Combine eggs and next 4 ingredients. Mix well, and pour over sausage. Cover and refrigerate at least 8 hours or overnight. Remove from refrigerator. Let stand 30 minutes. Bake, uncovered, at 325°. Sprinkle cheese over top. Bake an additional 5 minutes or until cheese melts.

# Oven Omelet

### 6 TO 8 SERVINGS

**½ stick margarine or butter**

**1½ dozen eggs**

**1 cup sour cream**

**1 cup milk**

**2 teaspoons salt**

**¼ cup chopped green onions**

**Chopped fresh parsley**

Heat oven to 325°. Heat margarine in a 13x9x2-inch baking dish in oven until melted. Tilt dish to coat bottom. Beat eggs, sour cream, milk, and salt in bowl until blended. Stir in onions. Pour into dish.

Bake omelet mixture about 35 minutes or until eggs are set but moist. Arrange omelet on large platter. Sprinkle with parsley.

*Homemade Christmas*

# Lasagna

8 TO 10 SERVINGS

1½ pounds ground beef

¾ cup chopped onion

1 (16-ounce) can tomatoes

1 (12-ounce) can tomato paste

2 cups water

1 tablespoon minced parsley

2 teaspoons salt

1 teaspoon sugar

1 teaspoon garlic powder

½ teaspoon pepper

½ teaspoon oregano

8 ounces lasagna noodles

16 ounces ricotta cheese

8 ounces mozzarella cheese

1 cup Parmesan cheese

Brown beef and onion. Add tomatoes (put through blender first) and next 8 ingredients. Simmer, uncovered, for 30 minutes. Cook noodles. In 13x9x2-inch pan, layer noodles, sauce, ricotta, mozzarella, and Parmesan cheese. Bake 40 to 50 minutes at 350°. Allow to stand 15 minutes before serving.

# White Bean Chili

### 4 TO 6 SERVINGS

1 large onion, chopped

1 clove garlic, finely chopped

¼ cup (½ stick) margarine or butter

4 cups cubed cooked chicken

3 cups chicken broth

2 tablespoons chopped fresh cilantro

3 tablespoons chopped fresh or 1 tablespoon
dried basil leaves

2 teaspoons ground red chiles

¼ teaspoon ground cloves

2 (16-ounce) cans great Northern beans, undrained

1 medium tomato, chopped

Blue or yellow corn tortilla chips

Cook onion and garlic in margarine in Dutch oven, stirring frequently, until onion is tender. Stir in remaining ingredients except tomato and tortilla chips. Heat to boiling; reduce heat. Cover and simmer 1 hour, stirring occasionally. Serve with tomato and tortilla chips.

# Standing Rib Roast

### 6 SERVINGS

**1 (6- to 8-pound) standing rib roast**

**2 large cloves garlic, split**

**1 large onion, thinly sliced**

**Salt and freshly ground pepper**

**1 ½ cups dry red wine, such as Bordeaux**

**or Cabernet Sauvignon**

**2 cups chicken stock or canned low-salt broth**

**Salt and pepper**

**Fresh parsley sprigs**

Preheat oven to 325°. Trim all but ¼-inch layer of fat from meat. Place meat bone side down in shallow roasting pan slightly larger than meat. Rub garlic over meat. Leave garlic in pan. Arrange onion around meat in pan. Sprinkle meat with salt and pepper. Roast meat 20 minutes. Pour ½ cup wine over meat.

Roast until thermometer inserted in center of meat registers 130° for rare, basting frequently with pan juices, and pouring about 3 tablespoons wine over meat every 30 minutes, about 2 hours 30 minutes. Transfer meat to heated platter, reserving drippings in pan. Tent meat with foil to keep warm. Skim fat off pan drippings. Set pan with drippings over high heat. Add stock and boil until syrupy, scraping up any browned bits and stirring frequently, about 8 minutes. Season with salt and pepper. Strain sauce. Garnish meat with parsley. Serve sauce separately.

# Stuffed Crown Roast of Pork

12 SERVINGS

**1 (7½- to 8-pound) pork crown roast (about 20 ribs)**
**2 teaspoons salt**
**1 teaspoon pepper**
**Mushroom Stuffing**

Heat oven to 325°. Sprinkle pork roast with salt and pepper. Place pork, bone ends up, in roasting pan on rack in shallow roasting pan. Wrap bone ends in aluminum foil to prevent excessive browning. Insert meat thermometer so tip is in thickest part of meat and does not touch bone. Place a small heatproof bowl or crumpled aluminum foil in crown to hold shape of roast evenly.

Roast uncovered until thermometer registers 160° (medium), 20 to 25 minutes per pound; or 170° (well), 26 to 31 minutes per pound. Prepare Mushroom Stuffing. One hour before pork is done, remove bowl or foil, and fill center of crown with Mushroom Stuffing. Cover only stuffing with aluminum foil during first 30 minutes.

When pork is done, place on large warm platter and allow to stand about 20 minutes for easiest carving. Remove foil wrapping; place paper frills on bone ends if desired. Remove stuffing to another bowl. To carve, cut roast between ribs.

## Mushroom Stuffing

**1 medium onion, finely chopped**
**⅔ cup margarine or butter**
**8 cups unseasoned croutons**
**1 tablespoon chopped fresh or 1 teaspoon dried sage,**
**thyme, or marjoram leaves**
**1 teaspoon poultry seasoning**
**1 teaspoon salt**
**½ teaspoon pepper**
**1 pound fresh mushrooms, sliced**
**2 medium stalks celery, chopped**

Cook onion in margarine in Dutch oven over medium heat about 3 minutes, stirring frequently, until tender. Stir in half of the croutons. Cook, stirring frequently, until evenly mixed and croutons are softened. Mix in remaining croutons and ingredients.

# Pork Tenderloin

### 8 SERVINGS

**¼ cup soy sauce**

**¼ cup bourbon**

**2 tablespoons brown sugar**

**2 (1- to 1½-pound) packages pork tenderloins**

**Mustard Sauce**

Combine first 3 ingredients in a 13x9x2-inch baking dish; add tenderloins. Cover and refrigerate at least 2 hours, turning meat occasionally. Remove from marinade; place on a rack in a shallow roasting pan. Bake at 325° for 45 minutes or until a meat thermometer inserted into thickest portion registers 160°. Serve with Mustard Sauce.

# Mustard Sauce

### 1⅓ CUPS

**⅔ cup sour cream**

**⅔ cup mayonnaise**

**2 tablespoons dry mustard**

**3 to 4 green onions, finely chopped**

Combine all ingredients; cover and chill.

## Roast Goose

### 8 SERVINGS

**1 (12-pound) fresh or frozen goose, thawed (neck,
gizzard and heart reserved for stock)**
**Salt and freshly ground pepper**
**1 tablespoon all-purpose flour**
**Fresh parsley sprigs**
**Stuffing**

Position rack in center of oven, and preheat to 400°. Season inside of goose with salt and pepper. Fill with Stuffing. Truss goose to hold shape. Place goose on rack set in large roasting pan. Rub skin with salt. Pierce skin (not meat) with fork.

Roast goose until skin begins to brown, about 30 minutes. Pour off fat from pan. Fill another large roasting pan with hot water. Place on floor of oven. Continue roasting goose 1 hour. Pour off fat from pan and reserve. Turn goose breast side down and continue roasting 1 hour.

Remove pan with water from oven. Turn goose breast side up and continue roasting until thermometer inserted in thigh registers 185°, about 45 minutes. (Cover breast with foil if needed.) Garnish goose with parsley. Serve with gravy.

## Stuffing

**2 tea bags**
**1 ½ cups boiling water**
**8 ounces pitted prunes**
**1 goose liver (reserved from goose)**
**2 tablespoons (¼ stick) unsalted butter**
**4 celery stalks, sliced**
**3 shallots, chopped**
**1 (8-ounce) jar whole roasted chestnuts**

Place tea bags in teapot. Pour boiling water over. Let steep 5 minutes. Place prunes in large bowl. Pour tea over. Let stand 30 minutes.

Drain prunes and chop coarsely. Transfer to medium bowl. Finely chop goose liver.

Melt butter in heavy large skillet over medium heat. Add celery and shallot and sauté 3 minutes. Add liver and sauté 2 minutes. (Can be made 1 day ahead. Cover and refrigerate. Bring to room temperature before using).

# *Sweet-Spicy Pork Kabobs*

**4 SERVINGS**

**½ pound boneless pork tenderloin or pork loin**
**16 to 20 (6-inch) bamboo skewers**
**¼ cup apple jelly**
**¼ cup taco sauce**
**1 teaspoon cornstarch**
**⅛ teaspoon garlic powder**
**Orange wedges (optional)**
**Corn relish (optional)**

Partially freeze pork (about 45 to 60 minutes). Soak bamboo skewers in warm water for 20 to 30 minutes. Cut pork into thin strips about ½ to ¾ inch wide and 4 to 5 inches long. Drain skewers. Loosely thread 1 or 2 pieces of meat on each, accordion style.

Combine jelly, taco sauce, cornstarch, and garlic powder in a small saucepan. Cook and stir over medium heat till thickened and bubbly. Cook 1 minute more.

Place kabobs on the unheated rack of a broiler pan. Broil 3 to 4 inches from the heat for 4 minutes. Brush meat with jelly mixture. Turn and broil 3 to 5 minutes more or until juices run clear, brushing again with the sauce when nearly done. Thread an orange piece on the end of each skewer, if desired. Brush again with sauce. Serve with corn relish, if desired.

# Beer Soup

### 8 SERVINGS

¼ cup (½ stick) unsalted butter

4 large onions, thinly sliced

Freshly ground pepper

4 cups beef stock or canned broth

4 cups dark beer

Salt

1 French bread baguette, cut into ½-inch-thick slices

¼ cup (½ stick) unsalted butter, melted

8 ounces Stilton or bleu cheese, crumbled

Melt ¼ cup butter in large saucepan over low heat. Add onions. Season with pepper. Press round piece of foil over onions. Cover pan with lid, and cook until onions are very soft, stirring occasionally, about 20 minutes. Remove lid and foil. Increase heat to medium and cook until onions are dark golden brown, stirring occasionally, about 25 minutes. Add stock and beer, and bring to boil. Reduce heat, and simmer 30 minutes. Season with salt and pepper. (Can be prepared 2 days ahead. Cover tightly and refrigerate.)

Preheat oven to 350°. Arrange bread slices on large cookie sheet. Brush melted butter over. Bake until crisp and golden brown, about 10 minutes. (Can be prepared 1 day ahead. Cool. Store airtight in plastic bag.)

Preheat broiler. Place 3 croutons in bottom of each of eight 1½-cup individual flameproof soup crocks. Bring soup to boil. Ladle over croutons. Sprinkle cheese on top. Broil until cheese bubbles and begins to brown, about 2 minutes. Serve immediately.

# Seafood Benedict

1 SERVING

**2 toasted crumpets or English muffins**

**4 ounces smoked salmon**

**2 poached eggs**

**Hollandaise Sauce**

Place crumpets on plate. Place thin sliced smoked salmon onto crumpets. Arrange poached eggs on top of salmon. Pour a generous serving of Hollandaise Sauce on top.

## Hollandaise Sauce

**⅛ cup butter or margarine**

**1 teaspoon lemon juice**

**1 egg yolk, well beaten**

**1 tablespoon evaporated milk**

**Dash of salt**

**¼ teaspoon ground chili powder**

Melt butter in saucepan. Stir in remaining ingredients, mixing well after each addition. Stir until mixture thickens. Serve warm.

## Creamy Peanut Soup

6 SERVINGS

**1 cup chopped celery**

**1 small onion, chopped**

**¼ cup butter or margarine**

**2 tablespoons flour**

**2 cups chicken broth**

**1 cup milk**

**1 cup heavy cream**

**1 cup peanut butter**

**Salt and pepper to taste**

Brown celery and onion in butter until tender. Add flour and broth; bring to a boil. Add milk and cream. Strain. Add peanut butter, and simmer for 5 minutes. Season with salt and pepper.

# Chicken Enchilada Casserole

8 TO 10 SERVINGS

1 (3- to 4-pound) chicken

1 carrot, sliced

¼ cup chopped parsley

1 stalk celery, sliced

1 ½ teaspoons salt

Black pepper to taste

4 tablespoons olive oil

1 small onion, chopped

4 (4-ounce) cans green chiles, chopped

¼ teaspoon cumin

Salt and pepper to taste

2 cups chicken broth

Cooking oil

16 corn tortillas

1 pound Cheddar cheese, grated

½ pound Monterey Jack cheese, grated

Sour cream

Sliced ripe olives

Place chicken in large pot with carrot, parsley, celery, 1½ teaspoons salt, and black pepper to taste. Bring to a boil, reduce heat, and simmer until chicken is tender, about 1½ hours. Cool, debone chicken, and cut into bite-size pieces. Strain broth, and set aside 2 cups.

Heat olive oil in large skillet; lightly sauté onion and garlic. Add green chiles, cumin, salt, pepper, and chicken broth. Simmer 20 minutes; then set aside. Heat cooking oil in a large skillet. Fry tortillas, one at a time, a half minute on each side. Drain well. In a 13x9x2-inch dish, layer tortillas, chicken, sauce, and cheese (save one-third of the cheese for the top). Spread sour cream on top; then sprinkle with cheese and olives. Bake in 350° oven for about 45 minutes.

# Salads & Side Dishes

## Colorful Christmas Coleslaw

### 6 SERVINGS

1 cup shredded green cabbage

1 cup shredded red cabbage

½ cup shredded red onion

½ cup thinly sliced green onion

¾ cup mayonnaise

1 teaspoon black pepper

1 teaspoon caraway seeds

Combine first four ingredients, mixing well for even distribution. Blend in mayonnaise, pepper, and caraway seeds. Chill before serving.

## Layered Holiday Salad

4 SERVINGS

**3 medium tomatoes, sliced**

**1 small bunch escarole, torn**

**1 medium red onion, sliced**

**2 medium zucchini, sliced**

**6 ounces radishes, halved**

**1 head broccoli, cut into bite-size pieces**

**1 cup diced red bell pepper**

**Oil and vinegar dressing**

Layer first 7 ingredients in order above in a large glass bowl. Add dressing.

## Crumbly Corn & Rice Dressing

8 SERVINGS

**½ cup water**

**¼ cup butter or margarine**

**¼ cup chopped celery**

**1 tablespoon minced onion**

**1 tablespoon minced parsley**

**1 cup herb-seasoned breadcrumbs**

**1 cup cooked corn**

**1 cup cooked rice**

Heat water, butter, celery, onion, and parsley in large saucepan until butter melts. Stir in breadcrumbs until well moistened, adding more water if necessary. Add corn and rice; mix well. Serve warm.

# Savory Acorn Squash

4 SERVINGS

**1 tablespoon margarine**

**¼ cup honey**

**1 tablespoon cinnamon**

**2 cooked acorn squash, halved**

Melt margarine. Stir in honey and cinnamon. Drizzle mixture over warm acorn squash. Serve immediately.

# Italian Eggplant

4 SERVINGS

**Nonstick cooking spray**

**1 medium-size eggplant, sliced ½ inch thick**

**½ cup Italian seasoned breadcrumbs**

**1 cup tomato sauce**

**4 ounces shredded nonfat mozzarella cheese**

Spray a baking sheet with cooking spray. Preheat oven to 400°. Moisten eggplant slices with water, coat with breadcrumbs, and bake for 15 minutes. Remove from oven, and top each eggplant slice with 1 tablespoon each tomato sauce and shredded cheese. Return to oven, and continue baking until eggplant is fork tender and cheese is melted.

# Green Beans with Pimiento

### 4 SERVINGS

1 teaspoon margarine

1 clove garlic, minced

⅛ teaspoon black pepper

1 tablespoon minced onion

2 cups green beans

1 jar pimiento, drained and chopped

2 teaspoons lemon juice

Melt margarine in nonstick pan over medium heat. Add garlic, pepper and onion; then add green beans, cooking until beans are warm and tender. Stir in pimiento, reduce heat, cover and cook until pimiento is warm. Sprinkle with lemon juice before serving.

In Ossun, Louisiana, the John B. Sonnier family has passed along this memory for generations. On Christmas Eve, the family's fireplace would be the center of Yuletide activity. A row of children's shoes, especially cleaned and polished to a high luster, would sit patiently waiting for the arrival of Santa Claus. (In most large Cajun families, the shoes that waited in great expectation back then might have been each child's only pair.) What a wonderful surprise in the morning to find Santa had placed a toy or perhaps fruit or candy in each pair of shoes.

—Bruce Gauthier
Breaux Bridge, La.

All Cajun Food Company

# Christmas Flecked Potatoes

### 4 SERVINGS

**4 medium potatoes, peeled, boiled and drained**

**¼ cup milk**

**1 tablespoon butter or margarine**

**1 small red onion**

**2 tablespoons chopped chives**

**¼ teaspoon white pepper**

Cut potatoes in quarters and mash to a smooth consistency. Blend in milk and butter until smooth. Stir in red onion, chives, and white pepper. Serve warm.

# Macaroni & Cheese

### 8 SERVINGS

**1 (1-pound) box elbow macaroni**

**2 tablespoons butter or margarine**

**3 tablespoons flour**

**1 teaspoon pepper**

**2 cups milk**

**½ cup shredded reduced-fat sharp Cheddar cheese**

**1 (10½-ounce) package broccoli flowerets**

Cook macaroni according to directions. In large saucepan, melt butter over medium-low heat. Add flour and pepper, stirring to create a smooth paste. Add milk slowly; cook over medium-low heat until white sauce thickens. Add cheese, and stir to melt; mix evenly. Drain macaroni, and place in large casserole dish. Combine broccoli and Cheddar cheese sauce with macaroni. Cover and bake in a 350° oven for 30 minutes. Let stand for 15 minutes before serving.

# Black-eyed Peas

6 TO 8 SERVINGS

1 pound smoked sausage, cut crosswise into ¼-inch
slices
½ pound diced ham
2 tablespoons vegetable oil
1 cup chopped onion
½ cup chopped green pepper
1 (15-ounce) can black-eyed peas, drained
½ teaspoon chopped jalapeño peppers
Salt and pepper to taste
Hot sauce (optional)

In a heavy saucepan, brown the sausage and ham in the oil. Add the onion and green pepper, and cook for about 4 to 5 minutes, or until wilted. Add the black-eyed peas and jalapeño peppers; simmer over medium-low heat for about 30 minutes. Add salt and pepper to taste; cook for 10 minutes more.

Serve over fluffy steamed white rice. Or, better yet, make a jambalaya of sorts by mixing the pea mixture with about 4 cups of cooked rice. If the mixture is too dry, add a little chicken broth to moisten.

## Smothered Cabbage

ABOUT 6 SERVINGS

1 large head of cabbage, cored and coarsely chopped

1 cup chopped ham

1 cup chopped onion

1 tablespoon vegetable oil

1 teaspoon sugar

Salt, cayenne pepper, and black pepper to taste

In a large heavy pot, cook the cabbage, ham, and onion in vegetable oil over medium heat, until onions are wilted (about 5 minutes). Add the sugar, salt, cayenne, and black pepper to taste; cook about 30 minutes, or until cabbage is tender. Stir occasionally during cooking.

## Broccoli Rice

12 SERVINGS

1 1/4 cups rice

1/2 cup chopped onions

1/2 cup chopped celery

1/2 stick butter

1 (10 3/4-ounce) can cream of chicken soup

1 small jar process cheese spread

1 package frozen chopped broccoli

1/4 cup breadcrumbs

1/4 teaspoon paprika

Cook rice and set aside. Cook chopped onion and celery in butter until tender. Add cream of chicken soup and small jar of cheese whiz to onion and celery mixture. Cook frozen chopped broccoli according to package directions. After broccoli is cooked, mix broccoli, cheese mixture and cooked rice together. Place in a casserole dish. Sprinkle breadcrumbs and paprika on top of casserole. Place in the oven at 350° for 30 minutes.

# Crawfish Cornbread Dressing

1 cup cornmeal

1 cup flour

¼ cup sugar

3 tablespoons baking powder

2 tablespoons salt

1 egg

1 cup milk

¼ cup corn oil

2 large onions, chopped

1 stalk celery, chopped

1 bell pepper, chopped

2 cloves garlic, minced

1 pound peeled crawfish tails

1 can Rotel tomatoes

1 (10¾-ounce) can cream of chicken soup

1 tablespoon flour

Dash Worcestershire sauce

Salt, black pepper, red pepper

Onion tops, parsley

1 large onion, chopped

1 stalk celery, chopped

2 tablespoons margarine

Chicken broth

1½ tablespoons mustard

Thyme, salt and pepper to taste

Mix together cornmeal, 1 cup flour, ¼ cup sugar, baking powder, and salt. Stir in egg, milk, and corn oil. When ingredients are well mixed, pour into a greased 9-inch pan. Bake for 20 minutes at 425°.

In a heavy pot, sauté onion, celery, bell pepper, and garlic for 30 minutes or until well cooked. When sautéed vegetables are soft, add peeled crawfish tails, tomatoes, cream of chicken soup, and 1 tablespoon flour. Stir in Worcestershire, salt, black pepper, and red pepper to taste. Cook for about 15 minutes; then add onion tops and parsley as desired. Let simmer an additional 15 minutes; set aside.

❧ Sauté other chopped onion and celery stalk in margarine in microwave on High for about 1 minute. Place mixture in a large bowl with broken cornbread pieces, adding chicken broth to moisten. Stir in mustard, thyme, and salt and pepper to taste. Add crawfish mixture. Pour dressing into baking dish, and place in oven for about 30 minutes at 350°.

# Mixed Fruit With Honey Almond Sauce

**6 TO 8 SERVINGS**

**Fruit**

**Lemon juice**

**1 (8-ounce) package cream cheese, softened**

**¼ cup milk**

**2 tablespoons honey**

**¼ teaspoon almond extract**

❧ Select several types of fresh fruits with varying textures. Wash, peel, core, and cut into bite-size pieces. Mix the fruit in a large bowl, and toss with freshly squeezed lemon juice; set aside.

❧ Place cream cheese in a small bowl. Use electric mixer to soften; add milk, honey, and almond extract. Blend until smooth.

❧ Serve fruit in individual bowls; top with sauce. The sauce can also be tossed with a large bowl of fruit before serving.

## Rosemary Potatoes

4 TO 6 SERVINGS

**4 large red potatoes**

**⅛ cup olive oil**

**1 teaspoon chopped garlic**

**1 tablespoon chopped rosemary**

**Salt and pepper to taste**

Thinly slice potatoes. Mix together olive oil, garlic, and rosemary. Pour over potatoes, and toss until potatoes are evenly coated. Cover microwave-safe dish with plastic wrap. Puncture two holes in the plastic wrap for ventilation. Microwave on medium to high for 12 minutes. Check to make certain potatoes are soft. Remove plastic wrap, and place potatoes under broiler to brown. Toss and brown potatoes again. Add salt and pepper to taste.

## Potato Latkes

14 TO 16 LATKES

**2 large potatoes**

**½ onion**

**2 eggs**

**¼ cup flour**

**1 teaspoon salt**

**Oil for frying**

Wash, scrub and cut potatoes into proper size for food processor or blender. Do not peel. Add all ingredients to processor or blender using stop and start until well blended, but not too fine. Pour into bowl. Heat oil in skillet. Drop by tablespoon into hot skillet and fry on both sides until brown.

To freeze: Spread latkes singly on a cookie sheet. When frozen, place in a plastic bag and return to freezer. To serve: place frozen latkes on cookie sheet and heat at 450° for approximately 7 to 10 minutes.

**Min Leonard**
*California Kosher*

# Garlic Mashed Potatoes

6 SERVINGS

**2 to 3 large baking potatoes, scrubbed**

**4 cloves garlic, unpeeled**

**½ cup milk**

**1 tablespoons butter**

**¼ teaspoon ground nutmeg**

**1 small egg, beaten**

**Salt and fresh ground black pepper to taste**

**2 tablespoons Cheddar cheese, grated**

Place potatoes and garlic in large saucepan, and cover with cold salted water. Bring to a boil over high heat; then cover and reduce heat. Simmer until potatoes are tender, about 45 minutes. Drain the potatoes and garlic. Peel the potatoes, and squeeze the garlic from their skins. Return potatoes and garlic to pan, and mash.

Preheat broiler. Heat milk, and add butter and nutmeg to milk. Stir until butter melts. Add milk gradually to potatoes, stirring well. Add the egg, and blend well. Salt and pepper to taste.

Transfer mixture to a 9-inch baking pan. Smooth top with a spatula, and sprinkle with cheese. Broil until nicely done.

## Praline Sweet Potato Casserole

8 TO 10 SERVINGS

**3 cups cooked mashed sweet potatoes**

**2 eggs**

**1 cup sugar**

**½ stick butter**

**1 teaspoon vanilla**

**½ cup milk**

**½ stick butter**

**½ cup packed light brown sugar**

**½ cup chopped pecans**

**⅓ cup flour**

Combine mashed sweet potatoes, eggs, sugar, ½ stick butter, 1 teaspoon vanilla, and ½ cup milk; set aside in 13x9x2-inch baking pan. Mix ½ stick butter, brown sugar, pecans, and flour. Crumble over top of casserole.

Bake at 350° for 35 to 45 minutes. Topping should be brown. This may be done a day ahead, refrigerated and bake 2 or 3 hours before serving.

## Cranberry Sweet Potatoes

4 SERVINGS

**¼ cup orange juice**

**¼ cup sugar**

**1 cup chopped cranberries**

**4 medium-size sweet potatoes, cooked and sliced**

Preheat oven to 400°. Combine orange juice, sugar, and cranberries. In casserole dish, layer sweet potatoes and berry mixture, alternating layers to the top. Cover and bake until thoroughly heated, about 25 minutes.

# Min's Noodle Kugel

### 10 TO 12 SERVINGS

**8 ounces wide noodles**

**4 ounces butter or margarine**

**6 eggs**

**1 cup sour cream**

**1 cup cottage cheese**

**½ cup sugar**

**½ cup milk**

**½ cup golden raisins, optional**

**½ pound dried apricots, optional**

***Topping***

**1 cup corn flake crumbs**

**1 cup brown sugar**

**¼ cup butter, melted**

Cook noodles in boiling salted water until tender. Drain and add butter. Set aside. Beat together eggs, sour cream. cottage cheese, sugar and milk. Add raisins or apricots or both. Add mixture to noodles. Pour into buttered 8x12-inch baking dish. Mix together topping ingredients. Sprinkle over kugel. Bake at 350° for one hour.

**Dotty Simmons**
*California Kosher*

# Squash Au Gratin

### 6 TO 8 SERVINGS

**2 pounds yellow squash**

**1 yellow onion, sliced in rings**

**1 (10¾-ounce) can cream of mushroom soup**

**2 cups grated American cheese**

**1½ cups crushed round buttery crackers**

Boil squash until tender with onion. When barely tender, drain well and mash just slightly. Fold in cream of mushroom soup. Salt and pepper to taste. Pour into a greased 11x7x1½-inch casserole dish. Top with grated cheese then cracker crumbs.

It was always a tradition for my brother and sister and I to wake up Mother and Daddy on Christmas morning. Daddy would get the camera ready. Then, and only then, could we go downstairs to the tree together. We'd go through our stockings first while Mother brought us juice; then Daddy passed out presents. My sister and I always competed to hide a present somewhere at the end to see who had the last present. Sometimes we'd be at Christmas brunch, and one of us would drag a present from under the couch (or wherever) and say "Ah-ha! I've got one more!" The rest of the family played along with the game. We continued this until last year (we are both in our late thirties now) when we were preoccupied watching her 2-year-old baby. I guess the game is over... but, then again, maybe last year was just a hiatus...

Karen Clements · Memphis, Tn.

# Cornbread Dressing

### 12 TO 14 SERVINGS

**Double Cornbread recipe (below)**
**3 to 4 bunches of green onions, sliced**
**4 large ribs of celery, diced**
**1 stick butter**
**6 slices bread, toasted and torn**
**1 to 2 teaspoons salt**
**½ to 1 teaspoon pepper**
**½ teaspoon sugar**
**2½ to 3 teaspoons sage**
**4 or 5 eggs**
**4 to 5 cups turkey broth**

Crumble cornbread and let dry. Sauté green onions and celery in butter. This may be done ahead and refrigerated. Just before stuffing turkey, combine dry ingredients, beaten eggs, sautéed vegetables, and broth. Taste and adjust seasonings. Stuff neck cavity, then abdominal cavity of turkey. Secure skin across cavities with tooth picks or a metal pin. Roast accordingly.

## Cornbread

**¼ teaspoon soda**
**1 cup buttermilk**
**1 cup cornmeal**
**¼ cup and 1 tablespoon flour**
**1 tablespoon baking powder**
**1 tablespoon sugar**
**1 teaspoon salt**
**1 egg, whisked a little**
**2 or 3 tablespoons water**

Preheat oven to 450°. Dissolve soda in buttermilk; set aside. Stir dry ingredients together. Add egg, buttermilk, and water. Grease an 8x8-inch pan or cast iron skillet. Heat until greased pan is hot. Pour batter into pan and bake 15 to 20 minutes.

# Snow-Dusted Trees

### 4 SERVINGS

1 teaspoon olive oil

1 pound broccoli, cut into flowerets and stems

½ teaspoon black pepper

1 tablespoon lemon juice

¼ cup Parmesan cheese

In a nonstick pan, heat olive oil over medium heat. Add broccoli, and sauté until tender. Stir in pepper; then sprinkle with lemon juice. Remove from heat, dust with cheese before serving.

# Marinated Red "Wreaths"

### 4 TO 6 SERVINGS

1 cup cider vinegar

1 tablespoon olive oil

1 teaspoon black pepper

½ teaspoon garlic powder

1 tablespoon oregano

4 medium-size tomatoes, sliced

Combine vinegar, olive oil, and spices. Place tomato slices in a shallow dish. Pour seasoned marinade over tomatoes; cover and marinate in refrigerator for 1 to 2 hours.

# Sugar and Spice

## And Chocolate Delight

Think back a moment to Christmas memories of childhood. What comes to mind? Baking Christmas cookies or fudge? Preparing an elegant dessert offered after Christmas dinner?

Adults look forward to the season to indulge in the sweets of their childhood traditions, and we all forego the diet for another slice of cake.

There is not a single holiday tradition that does not include some focus on sweets. Scandinavians bring us wonderful sweet breads, the French their Yule logs, the German tradition of cookies, and the Mexican flan.

Christmas is the season of sweet memories. In this chapter an array of memorable sugar and spice delights that can be created for your family to snack on around the tree, to bring to the office, to offer for a friend's holiday party, and to exchange with friends, both near and far.

As you prepare your families traditional holiday sweets, be sure to include several of the ones offered in this chapter.

# Cookies

## Chocolate Rum Balls

54 RUM BALLS

1 cup semisweet chocolate pieces

1/2 cup sour cream

1/2 pound vanilla wafers

1 cup sugar

1/4 teaspoon salt

3 tablespoons cocoa

1 tablespoon grated lemon rind

1 tablespoon grated orange rind

2 1/2 tablespoons lemon juice

1 1/2 tablespoons maple syrup

1/4 cup rum

1 cup pecans, finely chopped

Powdered sugar

Melt chocolate in double boiler; cool. Add sour cream. Refrigerate overnight. Form into about 54 balls, using 1/2 teaspoonful of mixture for each. Set aside to use for centers. Crush wafers; add 1 cup sugar, salt, cocoa, and rinds. Blend in lemon juice, syrup, rum, and pecans. Form balls the size of walnuts around chocolate centers. Roll in powdered sugar.

# Chocolate Chip Cookies

### 2 DOZEN

1 cup brown sugar

1 cup sugar

2 sticks butter, softened

1 cup oil

1 egg

2 teaspoons vanilla

1 teaspoon salt

1 teaspoon baking soda

1 teaspoon cream of tartar

3½ cups flour

1 cup flaked coconut

1 cup rolled oats

1 cup crispy rice cereal

1 (6-ounce) package chocolate chips

Combine ingredients in order listed; mix thoroughly. Chill dough for 10 minutes. Drop by teaspoonfuls on baking sheet. Bake at 350° for 12 to 15 minutes.

# Coconut Oatmeal Cookies

### 3 DOZEN

**1 stick butter, softened**

**1/3 cup sugar**

**1/3 cup packed brown sugar**

**1 egg, beaten**

**1/2 teaspoon vanilla**

**3/4 cup flour**

**1/4 teaspoon salt**

**1 teaspoon baking powder**

**1/4 cup milk**

**1/2 cup grated coconut**

**1 1/2 cups rolled oats**

**1 cup semisweet chocolate chips**

Cream butter with sugars until light and fluffy. Add egg and vanilla; mix. Combine flour, salt, and baking powder. Add the dry mixture alternately with milk to creamed mixture and blend. Stir in coconut, rolled oats, and chocolate chips. Drop by teaspoonfuls onto lightly greased baking sheet. Bake at 375° for 10 to 12 minutes.

# Lemon Tea Cookies

### 3 DOZEN

1 ½ teaspoons vinegar

½ cup milk

½ cup butter, softened

¾ cup sugar

1 egg

1 teaspoon shredded lemon peel

1 ¾ cups sifted all-purpose flour

1 teaspoon baking powder

¼ teaspoon baking soda

¼ teaspoon salt

¾ cup sugar

¼ cup lemon juice

Stir vinegar into milk. Cream butter and sugar until light and fluffy. Beat in egg and lemon peel. Sift together flour, baking powder, baking soda, and salt; add to creamed mixture alternately with milk, beating after each addition.

Drop by teaspoonfuls 2 inches apart on ungreased cookie sheet. Bake at 350° for 12 to 14 minutes. Remove from cookie sheet, and cool on wire rack.

For lemon glaze, blend ¾ cup sugar and lemon juice; brush on top of cookies while hot.

# Cheesecake Bars

### 16 BARS

⅓ cup packed light brown sugar

1 cup flour

½ cup chopped walnuts

⅓ cup butter, melted

1 (8-ounce) package cream cheese, softened

¼ cup sugar

1 egg

2 tablespoons milk

1 tablespoon fresh lemon juice

1 teaspoon vanilla

2 teaspoons grated lemon rind

Combine sugar, flour, and walnuts. Stir in butter. Reserve ⅓ cup of mixture. Pat remaining mixture into greased 8x8-inch pan. Bake at 350° for 15 minutes.

Beat cream cheese and sugar until smooth. Stir in remaining ingredients. Pour over crust, and sprinkle remaining ⅓ cup crumbs on top. Bake 25 minutes until set; cool. Cut into 2-inch squares.

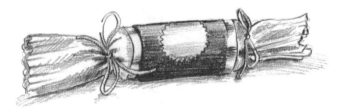

# *Peanut Kisses*

### 3 DOZEN

**1 stick butter, softened**

**½ cup sugar**

**½ cup brown sugar**

**½ cup peanut butter**

**1 egg**

**2 tablespoons milk**

**1 teaspoon vanilla**

**1¾ cups flour**

**1 teaspoon soda**

**½ teaspoon salt**

**Sugar**

**36 chocolate kisses**

Cream butter, sugars, and peanut butter together. Add egg, milk, and vanilla; beat well. Sift flour, soda and salt; combine with peanut butter mixture, and shape into balls using about 1 teaspoonful. Roll in sugar and bake on ungreased cookie sheet at 375° for 8 minutes. Remove and press a chocolate kiss on each ball until ball is flattened. Bake 3 to 4 minutes longer.

*Homemade Christmas*

# Caramel Meringue Squares

1 ½ DOZEN

1 ¼ cups sifted cake flour

1 ½ cups light brown sugar, divided

2 eggs, separated

⅛ teaspoon salt

½ stick butter

½ cup chopped walnuts, divided

1 cup caramels, cut up

Combine flour, ½ cup sugar, unbeaten egg yolks, and salt. Cut in butter with pastry cutter until mixture resembles coarse crumbs. Press firmly into an ungreased 13x9x2-inch pan. Sprinkle three-fourths of nuts on top, and press into crust.

Beat egg whites until stiff; gradually add rest of sugar. Fold in caramel, and spread over crust. Sprinkle with remaining nuts. Bake at 300° for 30 to 35 minutes.

# Lime Treats

4 DOZEN

2 cups flour

½ cup powdered sugar

1 stick butter

4 eggs

2 cups sugar

Salt

⅓ cup fresh lime juice

Powdered sugar

Combine flour and ½ cup powdered sugar; cut in butter. Press mixture into a 13x9x2-inch pan. Bake at 350° for 20 to 25 minutes. While crust is baking, beat eggs until light. Gradually add sugar, salt, and lime juice. Pour over hot crust. Bake at 350° for 20 to 25 minutes until golden. Remove and sprinkle with powdered sugar while hot. Cool; cut into bars.

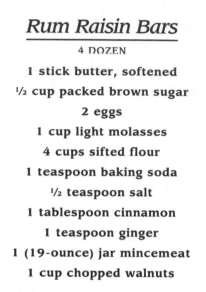

# Rum Raisin Bars

### 4 DOZEN

1 stick butter, softened

½ cup packed brown sugar

2 eggs

1 cup light molasses

4 cups sifted flour

1 teaspoon baking soda

½ teaspoon salt

1 tablespoon cinnamon

1 teaspoon ginger

1 (19-ounce) jar mincemeat

1 cup chopped walnuts

Cream butter. Beat in brown sugar and eggs. Stir in molasses. Sift flour with baking soda, salt, cinnamon, and ginger. Add dry ingredients to wet mixture. Beat until smooth. Stir in mincemeat and walnuts.

Spread mixture in a greased 15x10x1-inch baking pan. Bake at 350° for 30 minutes. Cool pan on wire rack, and spread frosting on top. Cut into bars.

## Frosting

### 1 (16-ounce) can vanilla frosting
### 1 tablespoon rum flavoring

Combine vanilla frosting and rum flavoring until smooth.

# *Mint Morsels*

### 3 DOZEN

**1 (6-ounce) package semisweet mint-flavored chocolate morsels**

**⅔ cup shortening**

**½ cup sugar**

**1 egg**

**¼ cup corn syrup**

**1¾ cups sifted flour**

**2 teaspoons soda**

**1 teaspoon cinnamon**

**¼ teaspoon salt**

**¼ cup sugar**

Melt mint-flavored chocolate morsels in double boiler. Cool. Combine shortening, sugar, and egg; beat until creamy. Blend in melted chocolate and corn syrup.

Sift together flour, soda, cinnamon, and salt; gradually stir dry mixture into chocolate mixture. Shape into balls. (Use level teaspoon for each.) Roll balls of dough in sugar. Bake at 350° for 12 minutes (check at 10 minutes). Let stand for a few minutes.

# Orange Slice Squares

4 eggs

¼ cup milk

1 pound box light brown sugar

2 cups flour

1 ½ cups candied orange slices, chopped

1 cup chopped pecans

Beat eggs, add milk and brown sugar, and beat well. Sift flour and add to mixture, reserving enough flour to mix with chopped orange slices and pecans. Fold into mixture. Pour batter onto a 15x10x1-inch well-greased cookie sheet. Bake at 400° for 20 minutes. Cool. Spread Icing evenly on top. Cut into squares.

## Icing

1 tablespoon butter, softened

3 tablespoons evaporated milk

1 tablespoon orange rind

2 cups powdered sugar

Combine all ingredients thoroughly.

# Red Plum Cookies

4 DOZEN

1 ½ sticks butter, softened

½ cup sugar

1 egg yolk, beaten

1 ¾ cups sifted flour

¼ teaspoon vanilla

Red plum jelly

Cream butter and sugar until light and fluffy. Add beaten egg yolk; gradually mix in flour. Add vanilla. Roll into small balls. Make indentation in each ball with finger, and fill with red plum jelly. Bake at 325° for 20 minutes.

# Raspberry Butter Cookies

### 100 COOKIES

**2 sticks butter, softened**

**3 heaping tablespoons sugar**

**2 teaspoons almond extract**

**2¾ cups sifted flour**

**Raspberry jam**

**Pecans**

**Powdered sugar**

Cream butter and sugar until light and fluffy. Add almond extract and flour; mix. Pinch dough, and roll into balls about 1-inch round.

Arrange on cookie sheet. Make dent in each ball, and fill with jam. Place pecan half on top. Bake at 350° for 15-20 minutes. Remove and cool. Roll in powdered sugar.

A live Christmas tree with all the lights and trimmings has always held some sense of magic for me. Ever since I was in grade school, I always wanted to help decorate the tree. After it was "up," we would turn out all the living room lights and light the tree. It was so beautiful and gave me a sense of inner peace. My mother taught me to sit back and reflect on the season... what it means to me and to value what I have and remember those less fortunate. We would sit for hours together, and sometimes I would sit by myself. Every year I do the same thing. Even though my tree might not always be live, the time in front of it is still valuable.

—Barbara Emigh · Memphis, Tn.

# Apricot Squares

### 4 DOZEN

1 stick butter

½ cup sugar

1 tablespoon grated lemon rind

2 eggs, separated

1 cup flour

½ teaspoon salt

¼ teaspoon baking powder

1 cup apricot jam

½ cup chopped walnuts

½ cup sugar

Powdered sugar

Cream butter, sugar, and lemon rind until light and fluffy. Add egg yolks, one at a time, beating after each addition. Sift dry ingredients together, and add to mixture.

Spread dough in greased 13x9x2-inch pan. Stir jam until smooth, and spread over dough. Sprinkle with walnuts.

Beat egg whites until foamy; gradually add sugar, and beat until stiff. Spread meringue over jam and walnuts. Bake at 350° for 45 minutes. Sprinkle with powdered sugar while warm. Cool before cutting into squares.

## Chocolate Chip Bars

2 DOZEN

4 eggs

3 cups brown sugar

1 1/3 cups oil

1 teaspoon vanilla

3 cups flour

3 teaspoons baking powder

Dash salt

1 cup chopped nuts

1 1/2 cups chocolate chips

Beat eggs and brown sugar until light and fluffy. Add remaining ingredients in order listed; mix well. Bake in 13x9x2-inch baking pan at 350° for 25 minutes. Cut into bars.

## Butter Pecan Turtles

24 BARS

2 cups flour

1 1/2 cups packed brown sugar, divided

1/2 + 2/3 cup butter, softened

1 cup chopped pecans

1 cup milk chocolate chips

Combine flour, 1 cup brown sugar, and 1/2 cup of butter; mix at medium speed for 2 to 3 minutes. Press into a greased 13x9x2-inch baking pan; sprinkle with pecans. Cook remaining brown sugar and butter over medium heat for 1 minute; stir constantly. Pour mixture over pecans. Bake at 350° for about 20 minutes or until caramel is bubbly and crust is golden. Sprinkle with chocolate; let stand until melted, then swirl chocolate over surface. Cool; cut into bars.

# Chocolate Marble Squares

### 3 DOZEN SQUARES

**1 (3-ounce) package cream cheese, softened**

**2 cups sifted powdered sugar**

**1 teaspoon vanilla**

**1 (6-ounce) package semisweet chocolate pieces, melted**

**½ teaspoon salt**

**¾ cup chopped marshmallows**

Blend cream cheese until smooth; mix in sugar, vanilla, chocolate and salt. Add marshmallows. Press into well-greased cookie sheet. Chill until firm. Cut into 1-inch squares.

# Lemon Pecan Slices

### 24 SLICES

**1 cup flour**

**1 stick butter, melted**

**2 eggs, beaten**

**1½ cups brown sugar**

**½ cup grated coconut**

**1 cup chopped pecans**

**2 tablespoons flour**

**½ teaspoon baking powder**

**½ teaspoon salt**

**2 tablespoons vanilla**

**1½ cups powdered sugar**

**Lemon juice**

Combine 1 cup flour with butter to make a smooth paste. Spread paste in 13x9x2-inch pan. Bake at 350° for 12 minutes. Combine the eggs and next 7 ingredients. Spread on top of the paste. Bake at 350° for 25 minutes. Cool. Combine powdered sugar and lemon juice until desired consistency for glaze, and spread on top. Cut into 1x2-inch slices.

# Butterscotch Bars

### 30 BARS

1 stick butter

1 ½ cups graham cracker crumbs

1 ⅓ cups coconut

2 (12-ounce) packages butterscotch chips

1 cup raisins

1 cup chopped walnuts

1 ⅓ cups sweetened condensed milk

Place butter in 13x9x2-inch pan; bake at 350° until melted. Remove from oven. Sprinkle crumbs over butter, and press down. Layer coconut and next 3 ingredients over crumbs. Drizzle with condensed milk. Bake at 350° for 20 to 25 minutes. Cool; cut into bars.

# Butterscotch Crispies

### 8 DOZEN

1 (6-ounce) package butterscotch morsels

1 stick butter

⅔ cup brown sugar

1 egg

1 ⅓ cups sifted flour

¾ teaspoon baking soda

⅓ cup chopped nuts

¾ teaspoon vanilla

Melt butterscotch morsels and butter in double boiler. Remove from heat, and beat in brown sugar and egg. Sift together flour and baking soda; stir into butterscotch mixture. Add nuts and vanilla. Chill. Shape into 12-inch roll. Wrap in wax paper; chill overnight. Slice dough thinly, and arrange on cookie sheet. Bake at 375° for 5 to 6 minutes.

## Banana Bars

4 DOZEN

1 stick butter, softened

1 ½ cups sugar

2 eggs

1 cup whole wheat flour

1 cup white flour

½ teaspoon salt

1 teaspoon baking soda

¾ cup buttermilk

1 teaspoon vanilla

3 ripe bananas, mashed

Cream butter, sugar, and eggs. Sift together flours, salt, and soda. Add milk and flours alternately to butter. Add vanilla and bananas; mix thoroughly.

Spread in greased jellyroll pan and bake at 350° for 30 minutes. Cool. Spread frosting evenly over top. Cut into bars.

## Frosting

1 (8-ounce) package cream cheese, softened

2 cups powdered sugar

1 teaspoon vanilla

1 stick butter, softened

Cream together all ingredients.

# Macaroons

### 2½ DOZEN

**1 (14-ounce) package flaked coconut**
**4 large egg whites, room temperature**
**1 cup sugar**
**1 teaspoon vanilla**

Granulate coconut in food processor; set aside. Beat egg whites until stiff peaks form. Add sugar slowly with beater at medium speed. Fold in coconut; fold in vanilla. Drop by teaspoonfuls onto a cookie sheet covered with brown paper. Bake at 325° for 18 minutes or until golden. Cool before removing.

# Fresh Apple Squares

### 36 SQUARES

**3 eggs**
**1¾ cups sugar**
**1 cup oil**
**2 cups flour**
**1 teaspoon baking soda**
**¼ teaspoon salt**
**1 teaspoon cinnamon**
**4 to 6 medium apples, pared and diced**
**1 cup raisins**
**¼ cup sifted powdered sugar**

Blend eggs, sugar, and oil until light and fluffy. Sift flour, soda, salt and cinnamon together, and stir into egg mixture. Beat well. Fold in apples and raisins; pour into a 13x9x2-inch greased and floured pan. Bake at 350° for 1 hour. Cool and sprinkle sifted powdered sugar on top. Cut into squares.

# Sunflower Cookies

4 DOZEN

2 sticks butter, softened

1 cup shortening

2 cups sugar

1 teaspoon vanilla

3 cups flour

1 teaspoon baking soda

1 teaspoon baking powder

1 cup sunflower seeds

1 cup flaked coconut

Cream butter, shortening, and sugar until light and fluffy; stir in remaining ingredients. Shape dough into 2 rolls, and refrigerate for 2 hours. Slice and arrange on cookie sheet. Bake at 350° for 10 minutes. Cool.

# Whole Wheat Peanut Butter Cookies

2 DOZEN

1 stick butter, softened

1/2 cup peanut butter

1/2 cup sugar

1/2 cup packed brown sugar

1 egg, slightly beaten

1/2 teaspoon vanilla

1 1/4 cups whole wheat flour

1/2 teaspoon baking powder

3/4 teaspoon soda

1/4 teaspoon salt

Mix all ingredients, and refrigerate overnight. Shape into balls; place 3 inches apart on greased cookie sheet. Mash down with fork. Bake at 375° for 10 minutes.

# Oatmeal Rocks

### 3 DOZEN

1 ¼ cups sugar

2 sticks butter

2 eggs, beaten

Pinch of salt

2 cups oatmeal

2 cups flour

5 tablespoons milk

1 teaspoon baking soda, added to milk

1 cup chopped raisins

1 cup chopped walnuts

Combine sugar and butter, and mix until light and fluffy. Add eggs. Mix together salt, oatmeal, and flour; stir into butter mixture alternately with milk and baking soda. Add raisins and walnuts; mix thoroughly. Dough should be stiff. Drop by teaspoonfuls onto greased cookie sheet. Bake at 350° for 12 to 14 minutes or until golden brown.

# Butter Balls

### 3 DOZEN

2 sticks butter, softened

½ cup sugar

2 cups flour

1 teaspoon cinnamon

1 teaspoon vanilla

2 cups cornflakes, crushed

1 cup pecans, finely chopped

¼ cup powdered sugar

Combine all ingredients except powdered sugar, and mix well. Roll into balls the size of a walnut. Place on ungreased cookie sheet and bake a 325° for 30 minutes. Roll in powdered sugar and cool.

## Lone Ranger Cookies

### 8 DOZEN

2 cups flour

1 teaspoon baking powder

1 teaspoon baking soda

½ teaspoon salt

1 cup shortening

1 cup sugar

1 cup packed brown sugar

3 eggs

1 teaspoon vanilla

¾ cup wheat germ

¾ cup corn flakes

1¾ cups crispy rice cereal

1¾ cups oatmeal

Sift flour, baking powder, baking soda, and salt together; set aside. Combine shortening and sugars; add eggs, and mix well. Add flour mixture slowly. Beat in vanilla and remaining ingredients. Drop mixture by spoonfuls onto greased baking sheet. Bake at 350° for 12 to 15 minutes.

## Sandies

### 20 DOZEN

2 pounds light brown sugar

2 pounds flour

5 sticks butter

3 eggs, unbeaten

3 eggs, beaten

Cinnamon and sugar mixture

Combine brown sugar and flour; work in butter with wooden spoon until well blended. Add 3 unbeaten eggs and work into dough. Roll out very thin on floured surface and cut with round cookie cutter. Place on greased cookie sheet. Brush on beaten egg mixture, and sprinkle with cinnamon and sugar mixture. Bake at 375° for 8 to 10 minutes until light brown. Cool.

# Crescents

**4 sticks butter, softened**

**1 pound cream cheese**

**4 egg yolks**

**4 cups flour**

**Powdered sugar**

Cream butter, cream cheese, and egg yolks until light and fluffy. Add flour; mix well. Roll out dough on surface dusted with powdered sugar. Spread filling over dough. Cut into 2-inch squares, and roll into crescents. Bake at 350° for 20 to 25 minutes.

## Filling

**4 egg whites, beaten**

**½ cup sugar**

**1 pound ground pecans**

**Drop of vanilla**

Beat egg whites. Add sugar, pecans, and vanilla.

*Until she died, my grandmother held Christmas Eve at her house every year; it was a great time to see all my aunts, uncles, and cousins. We always had a beautiful candlelight dinner with Big Moma's best china and the traditional turkey and mouthwatering homemade rolls and pecan pralines. Also, Mr. Snowman was always present; Big Moma made him out of two fish bowls and felt (see Page 25). Every Christmas she would fill him up with popcorn. He now graces my kitchen counter filled with popcorn. Even though he's at least 30 and a little ragged looking, he makes me smile thinking of those happy childhood memories.*

*— Sheila Thomas · Collierville, Tn.*

## Peanut Butter Brownies

16 BROWNIES

½ cup crunchy peanut butter

⅓ cup butter, softened

¾ cup packed light brown sugar

¾ cup sugar

2 eggs

2 teaspoons vanilla

1 cup flour

1 teaspoon baking powder

¼ cup salt

2 (6-ounce) packages semisweet chocolate morsels, divided

Combine peanut butter, butter, and sugars; beat until light and fluffy. Beat in eggs, one at a time, and add vanilla; set aside. Stir together flour, baking powder, and salt. Gradually stir dry ingredients into peanut butter mixture; mix well. Stir in one package chocolate morsels.

Spread batter into 13x9x2-inch baking pan. Sprinkle with second package chocolate morsels. Bake at 350° for 3 minutes; remove and spread melted chocolate topping evenly. Bake an additional 25 minutes. Cool. Cut into squares.

## Whippersnappers

30 COOKIES

1 (18-ounce) package lemon cake mix

1 (4½-ounce) carton whipped cream topping

1 egg

½ cup sifted powdered sugar

Combine cake mix, whipped topping, and egg; mix well. Drop by teaspoonfuls into powdered sugar; coat. Place on greased baking sheet, and bake at 350° for 10 to 15 minutes. Cool.

# Jumble Balls

3 DOZEN

2 sticks butter, softened
1 cup sugar
1 cup packed brown sugar
1 egg, slightly beaten
1 cup oil
1 cup oatmeal
1 cup crushed cornflakes
½ cup flaked coconut
½ cup chopped nuts
3½ cups sifted flour
1 teaspoon baking soda
1 teaspoon salt
1 teaspoon vanilla

Cream butter, sugars, and egg until light and fluffy. Add remaining ingredients in order listed. Form into 1-inch balls, and place on ungreased baking sheet. Bake at 350° for 8 to 10 minutes.

# Scotcheroos

5 DOZEN

1 cup light corn syrup
1 cup sugar
1 cup peanut butter
6 cups crispy rice cereal
1 (12-ounce) package semisweet chocolate morsels, melted

Combine syrup and sugar in saucepan; bring to a boil. Add peanut butter and cereal. Spread into bottom of greased 13x9x2-inch pan. Pour melted chocolate on top, and spread evenly. Chill until chocolate is firm. Remove and allow to come to room temperature before cutting into squares.

# Molasses Cookies

### 3 DOZEN

2½ cups sifted flour

2 teaspoons baking soda

2 teaspoons cloves

2 teaspoons ginger

1 teaspoon nutmeg

2 teaspoon cinnamon

1 cup sugar

¾ cup butter, softened

1 egg, beaten

4 tablespoons molasses

Sugar

Combine flour, baking soda, and spices; sift three times and set aside. Cream sugar and butter until light and fluffy. Add egg; beat well; add molasses and flour mixture gradually. Chill dough, and roll into balls the size of a walnut. Dip in sugar. Place sugar side up on greased baking sheet. Bake at 350° for 10 minutes. Cool.

*When I was 11, we packed our camper in Michigan and headed to Eudora, Mississippi, to spend Christmas with my sister. It snowed the whole way there, and the camper just kept swaying. Dad said it was just God pushing it along so that we would get there faster. Mother didn't think it was as much fun as Dad and I did. On Christmas day, Mother got diamond earrings, and I got turquoise butterfly earrings from Dad. It was a great holiday. Dad died the next June, and I wore the butterfly earrings to his funeral. I recently got married, and Mother gave me her diamond earrings to wear on my wedding day. I knew Dad was with me on my special day.*

*—Amy Coats · Southaven, Ms.*

# *Applesauce Cookies*

2½ DOZEN

½ cup shortening

1 cup sugar

1 egg

1 tablespoon vanilla

2 cups sifted flour

1 teaspoon baking powder

½ teaspoon baking soda

½ teaspoon salt

½ teaspoon cinnamon

½ teaspoon nutmeg

⅓ teaspoon cloves

1 cup applesauce

Cream shortening. Add sugar gradually and blend until light and fluffy. Add egg and vanilla. Sift dry ingredients together. Add shortening mixture, alternately with applesauce. Blend. Drop by heaping teaspoonfuls 2 inches apart onto greased baking sheet. Bake at 350° for 12 minutes. Cool on wire rack.

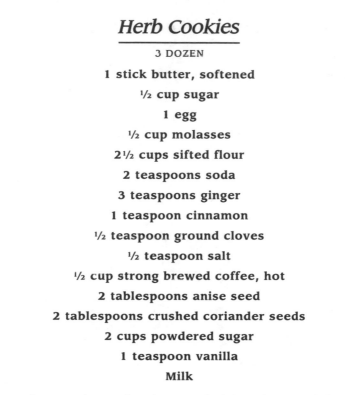

# Herb Cookies

### 3 DOZEN

1 stick butter, softened

½ cup sugar

1 egg

½ cup molasses

2½ cups sifted flour

2 teaspoons soda

3 teaspoons ginger

1 teaspoon cinnamon

½ teaspoon ground cloves

½ teaspoon salt

½ cup strong brewed coffee, hot

2 tablespoons anise seed

2 tablespoons crushed coriander seeds

2 cups powdered sugar

1 teaspoon vanilla

Milk

Cream butter and sugar; beat in egg and stir in molasses. Sift flour and spices together; add alternately with coffee to creamed mixture. Stir in anise and coriander seeds. Drop by teaspoonfuls onto greased baking sheet; 2 inches apart. Bake at 350° for 8 to 10 minutes. Cool. Frost with glaze of combined powdered sugar, vanilla, and enough milk for spreading consistency.

# Lemon Pecan Bars

**2 DOZEN SQUARES**

**1 cup sifted flour**
**1 stick butter, softened**
**2 eggs, beaten**
**1 ½ cups packed brown sugar**
**1 cup chopped pecans**
**2 tablespoons flour**
**½ teaspoon baking powder**
**½ teaspoon salt**
**1 teaspoon vanilla**
**1 ½ cups powdered sugar**
**Lemon juice**

Combine flour and butter until a smooth paste. Spread in 13x9x2-inch pan, and bake at 350° for 12 minutes. Combine eggs, sugar, pecans, 2 tablespoons flour, baking powder, salt, and vanilla. Spread on cake. Bake at 350° for 25 minutes. Cool. Spread with sugar thinned to spreading consistency with lemon juice. Cut into squares.

# Gingersnaps

3 DOZEN

1 ½ sticks butter, softened

1 egg

4 tablespoons dark molasses

1 cup sugar

2 cups flour

2 teaspoons baking soda

1 teaspoon ginger

1 teaspoon ground cloves

1 teaspoon cinnamon

Sugar

Combine butter, egg, and molasses. Add sugar. Sift together the flour, baking soda, and next 3 ingredients; add to sugar mixture. Bake on greased baking sheet at 375° for 10 to 12 minutes.

# Walnut Date Bars

2 ½ DOZEN

½ cup butter, softened

1 ¼ cups sugar

3 eggs, beaten

1 ½ cups sifted flour

½ teaspoon baking powder

1 cup coarsely chopped walnuts

1 cup diced dates

1 teaspoon vanilla

Cream together butter and sugar. Add eggs; beat to blend. Sift together flour and baking powder. Stir into egg mixture until well blended. Stir in walnuts, dates, and vanilla. Pour batter into greased and floured 13x9x2-inch pan. Bate at 350° for 25 to 30 minutes. Cool. Cut into bars.

# Forgotten Tea Cakes

16 TEA CAKES

¹/₃ cup butter-flavored shortening

¹/₂ cup sugar

1 egg

1 teaspoon vanilla

2 cups flour

2 teaspoons baking powder

¹/₄ teaspoon baking soda

¹/₄ teaspoon salt

¹/₄ cup buttermilk

Combine shortening and sugar; beat at medium speed of electric mixer until light and fluffy. Beat in egg and vanilla. Combine flour, baking powder, baking soda, and salt. Add alternately with buttermilk to creamed mixture at low speed. Mix well after each addition.

Roll dough to ¹/₂-inch thickness on lightly floured surface. Cut with floured 2¹/₂-inch cutter. Place on greased baking sheet. Bake at 375° for 7 to 10 minutes. Cool on wire rack.

# Poppyseed Cookies

4 DOZEN

3 eggs

1 cup sugar

³/₄ cup oil

Rind and juice of 1 orange

4 cups flour

¹/₄ cup poppyseeds

2 teaspoons baking powder

Salt

Beat eggs, and add sugar, oil, orange rind, and orange juice. Stir in dry ingredients. Roll out thin, and cut with cookie cutter. Bake at 350° for about 10 minutes.

# Anise Cookies

9 DOZEN

2 squares unsweetened chocolate

1 cup shortening

1 cup packed brown sugar

1 cup corn syrup

1 cup light molasses

2 eggs

1 cup sour cream

1/2 teaspoon cinnamon

1 tablespoon cardamom

1/2 teaspoon cloves

1/2 teaspoon allspice

1/2 teaspoon nutmeg

1 teaspoon baking soda

1/2 lemon, rind, and juice

1 teaspoon anise oil

9 cups flour, divided

Melt chocolate and shortening in double boiler. Combine all ingredients except for 2 cups of the flour with electric mixer. Work in last 2 cups flour to make soft dough. Chill overnight. Roll out thin on lightly floured surface, and cut out cookies with cookie cutters of your choice. Bake at 350° for 10 minutes. Cool.

# Chocolate Peppermints

### 18 MINTS

**2 sticks butter**

**2 cups powdered sugar**

**4 eggs**

**4 (1-ounce) squares unsweetened chocolate, melted**

**2 teaspoons vanilla**

**½ teaspoon peppermint extract**

**Pecans, toasted and chopped**

Cream butter and sugar until light and fluffy. Add eggs one at a time; beating well after each addition. Add the chocolate, vanilla, and peppermint extract. Sprinkle bottom of 18 muffin cups with toasted pecans. Fill cups with chocolate mixture. Freeze.

# Meringue Cookies

### 3 DOZEN

**2 egg whites, room temperature**

**⅛ teaspoon salt**

**⅛ teaspoon cream of tartar**

**¾ cup sugar**

**½ teaspoon vanilla**

**1 cup semisweet chocolate morsels**

**1 cup chopped walnuts**

**3 tablespoons crushed peppermint candy**

Beat egg whites at high speed until foamy. Add salt and cream of tartar, and continue beating until soft peaks form. Add sugar, 1 tablespoon at a time, beating well after each addition. When stiff and white, fold in vanilla, chocolate morsels, walnuts, and crushed candy. Drop by teaspoonfuls 1½ inches apart onto lightly greased cookie sheets. Bake 40 minutes at 250°. Remove and cool on wire rack.

# Gingerbread Men

3 TO 4 DOZEN

2 cups sugar

½ cup shortening

½ cup butter, softened

2 eggs

½ cup dark molasses

4 cups flour

2 teaspoons cinnamon

1 teaspoon ginger

1 teaspoon cloves

1 teaspoon nutmeg

1 teaspoon baking soda

¼ teaspoon salt

3 cups powdered sugar

1 teaspoon vanilla

4 to 6 tablespoons water

Colored sugars, raisins, citron, and
chocolate chips for decoration

Cream sugar, shortening, and butter. Stir in eggs, one at a time, blending well. Stir in molasses. Sift together dry ingredients; stir into sugar-egg mixture, mixing until thoroughly blended. Roll into a ball; wrap in wax paper. Chill 3 hours.

Roll out on floured surface to ¼-inch thickness. Cut out with gingerbread man cookie cutter. Place on greased cookie sheets. Bake at 325° for 10 to 12 minutes.

Mix powdered sugar, vanilla, and water for frosting. Spread with frosting. Decorate.

# Sleighbell Cookies

6 DOZEN

**2 sticks butter, softened**

**1 1/2 cups powdered sugar**

**1 cup sugar**

**1 cup oil**

**2 eggs**

**1 teaspoon vanilla**

**4 cups flour**

**1 teaspoon cream of tartar**

**1 teaspoon salt**

**1 teaspoon baking soda**

Beat butter, sugars, and oil until light and fluffy. Add eggs and vanilla; beat well. Add dry ingredients, and mix. Chill overnight. Roll into small balls and flatten. Bake at 375° for 10 minutes.

# Santa's Snacks

6 TO 8 DOZEN

**2 cups butter**

**2 cups sugar**

**4 cups unsifted flour**

**4 teaspoons cinnamon**

**1/2 teaspoon nutmeg**

**1 teaspoon ground cloves**

**1/2 teaspoon baking soda**

**1/4 teaspoon salt**

**1/2 cup sour cream**

**1/2 cup chopped nuts**

Cream butter and sugar until light and fluffy. Sift flour with spices, baking soda, and salt. Add to butter mixture alternately with sour cream. Add nuts. Knead. Shape into logs, wrap in wax paper, and chill overnight. Slice and bake at 350° for 10 to 12 minutes.

# Chocolate Snowballs

2 TO 3 DOZEN

**1 cup butter**

**½ cup sugar**

**1 ½ teaspoons vanilla**

**2 cups flour**

**Chocolate kisses candy**

**Powdered sugar**

Cream together butter, sugar, and vanilla. Add flour, and mix well. Chill 2 hours, and then shape into balls around chocolate kisses. Place on greased baking sheet. Bake at 375° for 15 minutes. Remove from pan, and roll in powdered sugar while warm.

# Christmas Wreath Cookies

6 DOZEN

**3 sticks butter, softened**

**1 cup sugar**

**2 teaspoons grated orange rind**

**2 eggs**

**4 cups sifted flour**

**Red candied cherries, chopped**

**Green candied cherries, chopped**

**1 egg white**

**2 tablespoons sugar**

Cream butter and sugar until light and fluffy. Add orange rind and eggs; mix well. Stir in flour. Chill dough. Break off small pieces; roll to pencil-size thickness, 4 inches long. Form into wreaths. Press bits of red and green candied cherries for holly berries and green leaves. Beat egg white until stiff; gradually beat in sugar. Brush wreaths with egg white mixture. Bake at 400° for 10 to 12 minutes until set, but not brown.

# Star Cookies

**2 DOZEN**

**7 egg whites**

**1 pound powdered sugar**

**1 tablespoon cinnamon**

**1 pound blanched almonds, cut fine**

**¾ cup flour**

**½ teaspoon baking powder**

Beat egg whites until very stiff. Add powdered sugar slowly. Remove ¾ cup of mixture for frosting; set aside. Combine cinnamon, almonds, flour, and baking powder. Add to sugar mixture. Roll out thin. Cut with a star cookie cutter. Dip in frosting. Arrange on well-greased cookie sheet, and bake at 200° for 10 minutes.

Every Christmas during college my grandmother and I would take a Saturday to go Christmas shopping together. One day I asked her about her favorite Christmas. She thought for a moment and then began the tale that no one else would hear but me. "I grew up in the Depression with my mother, brother and sister," she began. "One year we children decided to put our money together to buy mother a special gift. We had about 30 cents between us, but we headed to the thrift store and purchased a beautiful necklace. When mother unwrapped it, she began to cry, hugged us tightly, and said it was the most beautiful gift, besides her children, she had ever gotten." Now that grandmother is gone, I realize how precious our time was together, and that no gift on earth is worthwhile unless it is given from the heart.

— Josie Ware · Fayetteville, Ar.

# Mrs. Claus' Cookies

### 6 TO 7 DOZEN

**1 cup sifted flour**

**1 teaspoon baking powder**

**½ teaspoon salt**

**2 teaspoons ground cinnamon**

**½ teaspoon ground nutmeg**

**¼ teaspoon ground cloves**

**1 stick butter**

**½ cup packed brown sugar**

**1 tablespoon grated orange peel**

**½ cup evaporated milk**

**2 cups chopped walnuts**

**1 (6-ounce) package semisweet chocolate morsels**

**1 cup raisins**

Sift flour, baking powder, salt, and spices together. Cream butter; gradually add brown sugar. Mix in orange peel. Alternately add dry ingredients and evaporated milk; mix after each addition. Stir in remaining ingredients. Drop by teaspoonfuls onto lightly greased cookie sheets. Bake at 375° for 12 minutes. Remove cookies from cookie sheets, and cool on wire rack.

# Santa Claus' Whiskers

### 6 TO 7 DOZEN

**2 sticks butter**

**1 cup sugar**

**2 tablespoons milk**

**1 teaspoon vanilla**

**2½ cups flour**

**1 cup finely chopped red candied cherries**

**½ cup finely chopped walnuts**

**1 cup flaked coconut**

Cream butter; add sugar, and beat until light and fluffy. Add milk and vanilla; beat. Stir in flour, cherries, and walnuts. Shape into 7-inch rolls. Roll dough in coconut, coating well. Wrap in plastic wrap; chill overnight. Cut into ¼-inch slices. Bake at 375° on ungreased cookie sheet for 12 minutes until edges are brown.

Sometimes starting new traditions is a good idea. My mother passed away in September 1990. The first Christmas after that we all tried really hard to carry on the regular traditions, including the big meal she always prepared. Most of the day seemed okay — breakfast, exchanging gifts etc. — but dinner was awful. Nothing tasted right, and nothing felt right. We all decided the following year that we wouldn't try to recreate what would never and could never be the same again. So my father suggested we have an Italian Christmas Dinner. (There's no Italian heritage in our family, but it's our favorite type of food.) The second year went much better, so we have continued the tradition and add new items to the menu yearly. The old memories with Mom will never be forgotten, but we are building new ones as well.

—Kathy Brooks · Bartlett, Tn.

# Grandmother's Ginger Cookies

### 6 DOZEN COOKIES

**1 cup sugar**

**1 cup butter or margarine**

**2 eggs**

**1 teaspoon ginger**

**1 teaspoon cinnamon**

**4 teaspoons vinegar mixed with 3 teaspoons baking soda**

**1 cup molasses**

**4 to 5 cups all-purpose flour**

In medium bowl, beat sugar and butter until smooth. Stir in eggs, ginger, cinnamon, vinegar with soda, and molasses. Mix well. Stir in enough flour for a soft dough to form. Refrigerate about 1 hour or overnight.

When ready to bake cookies, remove about one-third of mixture, leaving remainder in refrigerator. Sprinkle surface with flour/sugar mixture. (This prevents working in too much flour, which will make cookies tough.) Roll ⅛- to ¼-inch thick, and use cookie cutters as desired. Carefully move to ungreased baking sheet. Decorate with colored sugars and candies before baking. Bake at 350° for 7 to 9 minutes or until cookies are set and slightly puffed. Remove immediately to wire cooling racks.

# Incredible Brownies

### 4 DOZEN

**4 (4-ounce) squares unsweetened chocolate**

**1 cup butter or margarine**

**2 cups sugar**

**1 cup all-purpose flour**

**4 beaten eggs**

**2 teaspoons liqueur of your choice or vanilla**

**1 cup semisweet chocolate pieces**

**1 cup chopped nuts**

Preheat oven to 325°. In a heavy saucepan, melt chocolate and butter, stirring constantly. Remove from heat. In a large bowl, stir together sugar and flour. Add melted chocolate mixture, eggs, and liqueur. Mix well. Stir in chocolate pieces and nuts. Spread batter in a greased 13x9x2-inch baking pan. Bake for 35 minutes or until edges are firm. (Center will be soft.) Cool 30 to 40 minutes on a wire rack before cutting. Chill at least 2 hours before serving.

# Sugar Cookies

### 5 DOZEN

**½ cup butter or margarine, softened**

**¾ cup sugar**

**1 egg**

**¾ teaspoon vanilla extract**

**2 cup all purpose flour**

**½ teaspoon baking soda**

**½ teaspoon salt**

Cream butter in a large mixing bowl; add sugar, beating until light and fluffy; add egg and vanilla, mixing well. Divide dough into thirds; roll each portion to ⅛ inch thickness on lightly floured wax paper. Cut with desired cutters. To bake, place 2 inches apart on a lightly greased cookie sheet. Bake at 375° for 8 to 10 minutes, or until lightly browned. Remove to wire racks to cool.

# Hugs and Kisses Cookies

ABOUT 5 DOZEN

2 1/4 cups all-purpose flour

1/2 teaspoon baking soda

1/4 teaspoon salt

1 cup light brown sugar, firmly packed

1/2 cup white sugar

3/4 cup salted butter, softened (or butter-flavored shortening)

2 large eggs

2 teaspoons vanilla extract

1 cup chopped pecans, walnuts, or macadamia nuts

1 1/2 cups white chocolate bar, chopped

Preheat oven to 300°. In a medium bowl, combine flour, soda and salt. Mix well with a wire whisk. In a large bowl with an electric mixer, blend sugars at medium speed. Add butter to form a grainy paste, scraping down sides of the bowl. Add eggs and vanilla, and beat at medium speed until light and fluffy. Add the flour mixture, pecans, and white chocolate, blending until combined. Drop by rounded tablespoons onto ungreased cookie sheets, 2 inches apart. Bake 20 to 22 minutes or until edges begin to turn brown. Use a spatula to transfer cookies to a cool flat surface.

# Brownies

### MAKES 48

**4 (4-ounce) squares unsweetened chocolate**

**1 cup butter or margarine**

**2 cups sugar**

**1 cup all-purpose flour**

**4 eggs, beaten**

**2 teaspoon coffee liqueur, brandy, or vanilla**

**1 cup semisweet chocolate pieces**

**1 cup chopped nuts**

Preheat the oven to 325°. In a heavy 1-quart saucepan, melt chocolate and butter, stirring constantly. Remove from heat. In a large bowl, stir together sugar and flour. Add melted chocolate mixture, eggs, and coffee liqueur. Mix well. Stir in chocolate pieces and nuts.

Spread batter in a greased 13x9x2-inch baking pan. Bake for 35 minutes or until edges are firm. (Center will be soft). Cool 30 to 40 minutes on a wire rack before cutting. Chill at least 2 hours before serving.

# Mexican Wedding Cookies

**1 cup powdered sugar**

**2 cups flour**

**2 sticks butter, softened**

**2 teaspoon vanilla**

**Pinch of salt**

**2 cups finely chopped nuts**

**Powdered sugar**

Mix first 6 ingredients together and form into small balls. Flatten balls and bake on ungreased cookie sheet at 325° until barely brown on bottom (about 12 minutes). Roll in powdered sugar.

# Candies

## Espresso Truffles

### 40 TRUFFLES

**12 ounces semisweet chocolate**

**4 ounces butter, softened**

**2 eggs yolks**

**4 tablespoons rum**

**½ cup heavy cream**

**40 espresso coffee beans**

**½ cup ground espresso coffee beans**

**¼ cup cocoa powder**

Melt chocolate in top of double boiler. Remove from heat, and beat in butter, 1 ounce at a time. Add yolks, rum, and cream; beat until smooth. Cover and refrigerate until hardened. Take 1 teaspoon at a time and roll into a 1-inch ball. Push a whole espresso bean into center of ball using toothpick. Fill in the hole with chocolate. Sift together the ground espresso and cocoa powder on a plate, and roll each truffle in the mixture. Keep chilled.

## Peanut Butter Bites

### 2 TO 3 DOZEN

**1 cup butter**

**1 cup extra crunchy peanut butter**

**3 cups powdered sugar**

**6 ounces semisweet chocolate chips**

Melt butter, and stir in peanut butter. Add powdered sugar, and mix until smooth. Press into 13x9x2-inch pan. Melt chocolate chips, and spread on top of peanut butter mixture. Chill for 15 minutes. Cut into bite-size pieces.

# Chocolate Butterscotch Crunch

### 3 TO 4 DOZEN

**1 (6-ounce) package butterscotch pieces**
**1 (6-ounce) package semisweet chocolate pieces**
**1 (3-ounce) can chow mein noodles**
**1 cup salted cashews**
**1 cup miniature marshmallows**

In a medium saucepan melt butterscotch and chocolate pieces over low heat, stirring occasionally. Remove from heat. Stir in chow mein noodles, cashews, and marshmallows. Drop from a teaspoon onto wax paper. Refrigerate until firm.

# Carob Candy

### 24 PIECES

**½ cup honey**
**½ cup creamy peanut butter**
**½ cup unsweetened carob powder**
**1 cup roasted soybeans**
**1 cup raisins**
**1 cup flaked coconut, divided**

In a saucepan stir together honey and peanut butter over low heat until melted. Remove from heat; stir in carob powder until well blended. Stir in soybeans, and raisins, and ¾ cup of the coconut until well coated. Press mixture into 9x5x3-inch loaf pan lined with wax paper. Sprinkle top of candy with remaining coconut. Cover; chill until firm. Cut into slices and then into squares. Cover and refrigerate.

# Bonbons

18 BONBONS

**1 (15½-ounce) package brownie mix**
**½ cup chopped walnuts**
**1 egg**
**1 tablespoon water**
**18 chocolate kisses, unwrapped**

Mix together brownie mix, walnuts, egg, and water. Wrap dough by rounded tablespoonfuls around each chocolate kiss; seal edges. Place on ungreased baking sheet. Bake at 375° until bonbons are set, about 8 to 10 minutes.

# Caramels

1¼ POUNDS

**1 cup sugar**
**1 cup light corn syrup**
**1 cup light cream**
**¾ cup butter**
**1 cup chopped pecans**
**1 teaspoon vanilla**

Place sugar, corn syrup, cream, and butter in large, heavy saucepan. Cook over medium heat, stirring constantly. When mixture starts to caramelize, lower the heat and cook, stirring constantly to 244° on a candy thermometer. Stir in pecans and vanilla. Pour into lightly buttered 8x8x2-inch cake pan, and allow to stand until firm. Turn the block of candy out of pan and mark off ¾-inch squares. Cut with sharp knife. Wrap caramels individually in wax paper.

# Almond Roca

### 40 PIECES

**2 cups sugar**

**¹/₂ cup cold water**

**1 pound butter**

**1 (16-ounce) package semisweet chocolate chips**

**¹/₄ cup finely chopped almonds**

Stir together sugar and water over medium heat. Add butter in pieces as it melts. Cook until mixture registers 300° on a candy thermometer. Pour into well-greased cookie sheet, and allow to set.

When cool, melt chocolate, and pour over hardened candy. Sprinkle with almonds while chocolate is still soft. After chocolate hardens, turn out candy, and pour chocolate on other side. Allow to harden. Break into pieces.

# Chocolate-Covered Turtles

### 24 TO 30 TURTLES

**1 ¹/₂ cups flour**

**¹/₄ teaspoon baking soda**

**¹/₄ teaspoon salt**

**¹/₂ cup butter, softened**

**¹/₂ cup brown sugar**

**1 egg**

**1 egg yolk (reserve white)**

**¹/₂ teaspoon vanilla**

**2 cups pecan halves**

**1 small package chocolate frosting mix**

Combine first 8 ingredients. Chill dough. Lay pecans in groups of 3 to 5 to resemble legs of a turtle. Take rounded teaspoons of chilled dough, and shape into balls. Dip bottom of ball into unbeaten egg white. Press ball onto nuts, leaving tips of nuts visible. Bake at 350° for 10 to 12 minutes. Cool. Make frosting mix according to package directions, and frost top of turtles generously.

# Candied Citrus Peel

**Peel from 2 grapefruits, cut into wide strips**

**½ cup light corn syrup**

**1 cup sugar**

**1 cup water**

Place the strips of peel in a saucepan, and cover with water. Boil for 10 minutes, and drain. Repeat 3 times using fresh water each time. Then cut peel into ⅛-inch strips. Combine corn syrup, sugar, and water; add peel, and boil gently until most of the syrup is absorbed (about 40 minutes). Drain. Roll peel in granulated sugar, and dry for 48 hours.

# Chalvah

### 20 PIECES

**1 cup ground sesame seeds**

**½ cup shredded coconut (unsweetened)**

**¼ cup honey**

**¼ cup wheat germ**

**⅛ teaspoon almond extract**

Combine all ingredients. Divide into two parts, and form 1-inch-thick rolls. Cut rolls into 20 pieces. Chill.

# Lincoln Logs

### 3½ DOZEN

**1 cup chunky peanut butter**

**2 tablespoons butter, softened**

**1¼ cups sifted powdered sugar**

**3 cups crispy rice cereal**

**Chopped peanuts**

Combine peanut butter, butter, and powdered sugar. Add cereal; mix well, and crush slightly. Shape into three 7x1¼-inch logs. Roll logs in peanuts. Wrap in plastic wrap and chill. Slice in ½-inch-thick discs.

# Martha Washington Candy

4 DOZEN

1 stick butter

2 pounds powdered sugar

1 small can evaporated milk

1 teaspoon vanilla

Cherries, pitted

1 square unsweetened chocolate, shaved

1 square paraffin

Pecans

Cream butter; add sugar gradually. Add milk and vanilla; mix. Pinch off small pieces, press flat and insert a cherry. Roll into balls. Melt shaved chocolate and paraffin in a double boiler until dark. Dip candy into hot chocolate mixture, and coat evenly. Top with a pecan.

# Maple Sugar Pecans

2½ CUPS

1½ cups sugar

½ cup milk

¼ teaspoon salt

1 teaspoon light corn syrup

1 teaspoon maple flavoring

2½ cups pecans

Mix sugar, milk, salt, and corn syrup. Cook until mixture registers 234° on a candy thermometer. Add maple flavoring and nuts. Stir until mixture starts to harden; then pour at once onto wax paper. Separate pieces with a fork. Cool.

# Fabulous Fudge

### 3 DOZEN

**3½ cups sugar**

**2 tablespoons light corn syrup**

**2 cups sour cream**

**6 tablespoons butter**

**6 ounces milk chocolate, broken in pieces**

**1 teaspoon vanilla**

Combine sugar, corn syrup, sour cream, and butter in a heavy 3-quart saucepan. Cook over medium heat, stirring often with a wooden spoon. Cook until mixture registers 254° on a candy thermometer. Remove from heat. Add milk chocolate and vanilla. Let stand 10 minutes. Stir until it begins to lose its sheen. Pour into a buttered 13x9x2-inch pan. Cool. Cut into squares.

One of my favorite memories of the holidays is cranberry sauce, one of the foods always served with holiday meals. Sometimes it was the canned variety, but other times, it was made with fresh berries. It was always served in the same cut glass bowl. The years of use have put their marks on the bowl—with chips gone from most of the edges. But even with its imperfections, that bowl always added an element of elegance to the table. The holiday table was never complete without it. All of my siblings are grown now, but we recently realized our unknown but clear memory of cranberry sauce.

—Glen Wimmer · Memphis, Tn.

# Old-Fashioned Popcorn Balls

### 13 TO 15 SERVINGS

**20 cups popped popcorn (about 1 cup unpopped)**

**2 cups sugar**

**1 ½ cups water**

**½ cup light corn syrup**

**1 teaspoon vinegar**

**½ teaspoon salt**

**1 teaspoon vanilla**

Remove all unpopped kernels, and put popped popcorn in a large roasting pan. Keep warm in a 300° oven. Combine sugar, water, corn syrup, vinegar, and salt in a buttered 2-quart saucepan. Cook until mixture registers 250° on a candy thermometer, stirring frequently. Remove from heat; stir in vanilla. Slowly pour mixture over hot popcorn. Stir until just mixed.

Butter hands and a coffee cup. Scoop up popcorn mixture, and shape into 2½-to 3-inch balls.

Note: A few drops of red or green food coloring can be added to sugar mixture for festive popcorn balls.

# Orange Morsels

### ABOUT 2 DOZEN

**½ cup orange juice**

**1 ½ teaspoons finely grated orange rind**

**1 ½ cups sugar**

**1 teaspoon corn syrup**

**¼ teaspoon salt**

**2 ½ cups pecan halves**

Combine all ingredients except pecans in saucepan; cook until mixture registers 238° on a candy thermometer. Add pecans, and stir until creamy. Quickly drop by teaspoonfuls onto wax paper. Allow to harden.

# Peanut Butterscotch Candy

### ABOUT 10 DOZEN

1 ½ cups flour

½ cup butter

¾ cup brown sugar

⅛ teaspoon salt

1 (12-ounce) package butterscotch chips

1 ½ tablespoons butter

1 ½ cups water

¼ cup light corn syrup

1 ½ cups salted peanuts

Mix together flour, ½ cup butter, brown sugar, and salt; cut with pastry cutter until mixture is crumbly. Pat into a 13x9x2-inch pan. Bake at 375° for 10 minutes. Combine butterscotch chips, 1 ½ tablespoons butter, water, and corn syrup in the top of a double boiler until melted. Add peanuts. Spread mixture over baked crust as soon as it is taken from the oven. Return to oven, and bake for 8 minutes at 375°. Loosen edges from sides of pan while warm. Cool. Cut into 1-inch squares.

# Tropical Balls

### ABOUT 3 DOZEN

1 (6-ounce) can orange juice concentrate

1 pound vanilla wafers, crushed

1 (1-pound) box powdered sugar

1 cup chopped unsalted cashews

Flaked coconut

Mix together all ingredients except coconut. Shape into balls, and roll in coconut. Chill.

# Old-Fashioned Peanut Brittle

1 TO 1½ POUNDS

1 cup light corn syrup

2 cups sugar

½ cup water

1 pound raw Spanish peanuts

2 tablespoons butter

2 teaspoons vanilla

2 teaspoons baking soda

½ teaspoon salt

Combine syrup, sugar, and water in saucepan. Heat slowly until mixture registers 230° on a candy thermometer. Add peanuts, and continue to cook to 300°.

Remove from heat. Add butter, vanilla, soda, and salt; stir until blended. Pour into well-buttered 15½x10½-inch jelly roll pan. Cool. Break into pieces.

# Divine Divinity

2 TO 3 DOZEN

2½ cups sugar

½ cup water

⅔ cup light corn syrup

¼ teaspoon salt

2 egg whites

1 teaspoon vanilla

Combine sugar, water, corn syrup, and salt in saucepan. Cook over low heat stirring constantly until mixture boils. Continue cooking without stirring until mixture registers 266° on a candy thermometer. Beat egg whites very stiff. Slowly pour mixture over egg whites, beating constantly. Continue beating until candy is very stiff and holds its shape when dropped from a spoon. Add vanilla. Pour in 8x8-inch buttered pan, and let stand until firm. Cut into small pieces.

## White Christmas Mix

5 DOZEN

**2 pounds white chocolate**

**2 cups Spanish peanuts**

**2 cups small pretzel sticks, broken**

Melt chocolate in double boiler. Stir in peanuts and pretzels. Quickly drop by spoonfuls on wax paper. (Mixture hardens fast).

## Cinnamon Fudge

ABOUT 3 POUNDS

**4 (1-ounce) squares unsweetened chocolate**

**3 cups sugar**

**2 teaspoons cinnamon**

**2 tablespoons light corn syrup**

**1¼ cups milk**

**4 tablespoons butter**

**1 teaspoon vanilla**

**2 cups walnut pieces**

Melt chocolate in saucepan on lowest heat. Stir in sugar, cinnamon, corn syrup, and milk. Increase heat to medium, stirring until sugar dissolves. Cook until mixture registers 238° on a candy thermometer.

Remove from heat; stir in butter, and then cool to 110° on a candy thermometer. Add vanilla, and beat until mixture begins to thicken. Stir in nuts, and continue to beat until candy holds its shape. Drop by teaspoons onto buttered wax paper. Cool into squares.

# Mint Sticks

### 3½ DOZEN

**1 (2-ounce) package unsweetened chocolate**

**½ cup butter**

**2 eggs, beaten**

**1 cup sugar**

**¼ teaspoon peppermint extract**

**½ cup flour**

**Dash of salt**

**½ cup chopped almonds**

**2 tablespoons butter**

**1 cup sifted powdered sugar**

**1 tablespoon cream**

**¾ teaspoon peppermint extract**

Slowly melt chocolate and ½ cup butter . Combine eggs, sugar, peppermint, and chocolate mixture. Add flour, salt, and nuts. Pour into 9x9-inch pan. Bake at 350° for 20 to 25 minutes. Cool.

For frosting, cream 2 tablespoons butter; add the powdered sugar, cream, and peppermint extract. Stir until smooth, and spread over chilled mixture. Refrigerate until cool. Cut into narrow sticks.

# Desserts

## Strawberry Delight

### 12 SERVINGS

1 (6-ounce) package strawberry gelatin

1 cup of boiling water

2 (12-ounce) packages sliced strawberries, thawed

1 (20-ounce) can crushed pineapple, drained

3 medium bananas, mashed

1 cup chopped nuts

1 (8-ounce) package cream cheese

1 cup sour cream

In a large bowl, stir gelatin in boiling water until dissolved. Add strawberries with juice, pineapple, bananas, and nuts. Pour half the mixture into 12x8x2-inch container, and refrigerate until firm.

Soften cream cheese, and combine with sour cream. Spread evenly over chilled layer. Spoon on remaining half of strawberry mixture. Chill, and cut into squares to serve. (Serve on lettuce leaves for a salad instead of dessert.)

# Pumpkin Bread

### 3 LOAVES

1 cup vegetable oil

3 cups sugar

4 eggs, beaten

1 large can pumpkin

1 cup chopped pecans

3½ cups flour

2 teaspoons baking soda

½ teaspoon salt

1 teaspoon cinnamon

1 teaspoon nutmeg

Mix oil, sugar, eggs, and pumpkin together. Combine all dry ingredients and pecans in separate bowl. Mix the dry ingredients and the oil mixture together. Cook in 3 (1-pound) coffee cans or 3 loaf pans; grease them well, and fill half full. Bake 1 hour and 15 minutes at 350°. Remove from baking pans or coffee cans immediately, and cool.

# Polvorones

### 5 TO 6 DOZEN

*These are similar to round sand tarts.*

1 cup soft butter

½ cup powdered sugar

1¾ cups flour

½ teaspoon vanilla

½ cup chopped pecans

Powdered sugar

Cream butter and ½ cup sugar together. Beat in flour, a little at a time. Add vanilla and chopped pecans. Shape into little balls, and bake on ungreased cookie sheets at 350° for about 15 to 20 minutes. When cool, roll in powdered sugar.

# Sour Cream Pie

### 6 TO 8 SERVINGS

**1 egg yolk**

**¾ cup sugar**

**½ teaspoon ground cloves**

**½ teaspoon cinnamon**

**2 tablespoons flour**

**1 cup sour cream**

**½ cup chopped raisins**

**1 (9-inch) pie crust, baked and cooled**

**1 tablespoon cornstarch**

**½ cup water**

**3 egg whites**

**6 to 8 tablespoons sugar**

Beat egg yolk, sugar, spices, and flour. Mix with sour cream. Cook in double boiler until thick (about 30 minutes). Stir in raisins. When cool, spread onto pie crust. Combine cornstarch and water in saucepan. Bring to a boil, stirring until transparent. Set aside to cool. Beat egg whites with electric mixer until stiff but not dry. Gradually beat in 6 to 8 tablespoons sugar; add cornstarch mixture, and blend thoroughly. Cover pie with meringue. Before serving, brown meringue under broiler.

# Squash Pie

**6 TO 8 SERVINGS**

1 cup Hubbard squash, cooked and strained

1 cup whole milk

½ cup sugar

½ teaspoon salt

1 egg

¼ teaspoon cinnamon

⅛ teaspoon cloves

⅛ teaspoon nutmeg

1 (9-inch) pie crust

Mix all ingredients in a bowl with an egg beater. Pour into an uncooked pie crust. Bake for 40 to 45 minutes in a 425° oven.

# Lemon Pudding

**6 TO 8 SERVINGS**

1 cup sugar

1½ cups water

6 tablespoons cornstarch

3 eggs, separated

1 (6-ounce) can frozen lemonade, thawed

1 tablespoon butter

⅛ teaspoon salt

Whipped topping (optional)

In large saucepan, combine sugar, water, and cornstarch. Over medium heat, stir constantly, until mixture thickens and becomes clear. Pour a small amount of hot mixture into egg yolks, and beat well. Add to hot mixture, and return to medium heat, stirring constantly for 2 to 3 minutes. Remove from heat. Stir in lemonade, butter, and salt. Mix well; set aside to cool.

Meanwhile, beat egg whites until soft peaks form. Blend into lemon mixture. Pour into serving dishes, and top with whipped topping, if desired.

# Chocolate Gravy

## 10 TO 12 SERVINGS

*This is best served hot over hot homemade biscuits.*

**2 cups sugar**

**4 tablespoons cocoa**

**1 stick butter or margarine**

**3 cups milk, divided**

Mix sugar, cocoa, and butter in large saucepan over medium heat. Add ½ cup milk; let mixture come to a boil, and cook for 10 minutes. Add the rest of the milk, stirring constantly until mixture comes to a boil. Reduce heat to simmer, and let cook for 30 minutes.


# Chocolate Tarts

## 12 SERVINGS

**8 ounces semisweet chocolate**

**⅓ cup sugar**

**2 cups heavy cream**

**12 baked tart shells**

**Whipped cream garnish**

To make filling, melt chocolate and sugar in a heavy saucepan; stir constantly until smooth. Add the cream, and continue stirring for 8 to 10 minutes until the mixture thickens. Let the mixture cool, but not set, before filling the baked tart shells. Refrigerate the filled shells for at least 4 hours until set. Decorate with whipped cream.

# Bev's Chocolate Mousse

### 8 SERVINGS

1 ½ pounds semisweet chocolate chips

½ cup prepared coffee

½ cup Grand Marnier (or liqueur of your choice)

4 eggs, separated

2 cups heavy cream, divided

¼ cup sugar

Pinch of salt

½ teaspoon vanilla extract

Fresh whipped cream (garnish)

Melt chocolate chips in a heavy saucepan over very low heat, stirring constantly. Add coffee, and then stir in liqueur. Cool to room temperature. Add egg yolks, one at a time, beating thoroughly after each addition. Whip 1 cup of cream until thickened; then gradually beat in sugar, beating until stiff. Beat egg whites with salt until stiff. Gently fold egg whites into whipped cream. Stir about one third of cream and egg mixture thoroughly into chocolate mixture. Scrape remaining cream and egg mixture over lightened chocolate base, and fold together gently. Pour into 8 dessert cups or serving bowl. Refrigerate for 2 hours or until set. At serving time whip remaining cup of cream until thickened; add vanilla, and whip to soft peaks. Top each serving with fresh whipped cream.

# Frozen Margarita Pie

### 8 SERVINGS

1 can frozen limeade

1 can sweetened condensed milk

1 package frozen whipped topping

1 teaspoon triple sec

1 (9-inch) graham cracker pie crust

Blend first 4 ingredients, and pour into pie crust. Freeze. Remove from freezer 20 minutes before serving.

# Hot Chocolate Soufflé

**8 TO 10 SERVINGS**

**¾ cup sugar, divided**

**½ cup unsweetened cocoa**

**⅓ cup flour**

**¼ teaspoon salt**

**1 ½ cups milk**

**¾ teaspoon vanilla**

**6 eggs, separated**

**¾ teaspoon cream of tartar**

In a medium saucepan, combine ¼ cup sugar, cocoa, flour, and salt. Stir in milk. Cook over medium heat, stirring constantly until mixture boils and is smooth and thickened. Stir in vanilla; set aside.

In a large mixing bowl, beat egg whites with cream of tartar at high speed until foamy. Add remaining sugar, 2 tablespoons at a time, beating constantly until sugar is dissolved and whites are glossy and stand in soft peaks. Thoroughly blend egg yolks into reserved mixture.

Gently, but thoroughly, fold yolk mixture into whites. Carefully pour into a 1½- to 2-quart soufflé dish. Bake in a preheated 350° oven until puffy, delicately browned, and soufflé shakes slightly when oven rack is gently moved back and forth, about 30 to 40 minutes. Serve immediately.

# Brandied Holiday Cakes

12 SMALL CAKES

Butter

1/3 cup margarine, softened

1 1/3 cups packed light brown sugar

1/2 teaspoon vanilla extract

2 large eggs

1 cup all-purpose flour

1 teaspoon baking powder

1/2 teaspoon salt

1/4 cup orange juice

2 tablespoons brandy

1 cup candied fruit, finely chopped

1/2 cup dates, finely chopped

1/4 cup dried apricots, finely chopped

1/3 cup sugar

1/3 cup orange juice

2 tablespoons brandy

Grease 12 muffin tins very generously with butter. Preheat oven to 350°. Place the softened margarine, brown sugar, and vanilla in a mixing bowl; cream well. Add eggs, one at a time, and beat well after each addition. Combine flour, baking powder, and salt. Add to the creamed mixture alternately with orange juice and brandy. Stir in fruits.

Fill each muffin tin almost to the top. Place a pan of hot water on bottom rack of oven. Place the muffin tins on middle rack. Bake for about 25 minutes. When cakes are done, remove from oven and cool for 10 minutes. Using a 2-tined fork, prick tops of cakes lightly. Combine remaining 3 ingredients in a saucepan. Heat over low heat. Pour over cakes.

# Truffles

2 DOZEN

**6 ounces semisweet chocolate**

**¼ cup butter**

**3 tablespoons whipping cream**

**1 egg yolk, beaten**

**3 tablespoons rum, brandy, or whipping cream**

Combine semisweet chocolate, butter and 3 tablespoons whipping cream in a heavy 2-quart saucepan. Cook over low heat until chocolate is melted. Remove from heat. Gradually stir about half of the hot mixture into the beaten egg yolk. Return egg mixture to saucepan. Cook over medium heat, stirring until thickened. Stir in rum, brandy, or whipping cream. Transfer to a small mixing bowl. Chill until mixture is room temperature, about 1 hour. Beat the cooled mixture about 2 minutes. Chill about 15 more minutes. Drop 1 tablespoon of chocolate on a baking sheet; chill. Roll into smooth balls. Dip in cocoa, powdered sugar, and nuts. Chill.

# Mother's Coconut Cake

10 TO 12 SERVINGS

*This recipe needs to made two to three days before serving.*

**1 (18.25-ounce) package golden butter cake mix**

**2 cups sugar**

**12 ounces frozen shredded coconut, thawed**

**2 cups sour cream**

**2 cups whipped topping**

Prepare cake according to package directions; bake in 2 round pans. When cake has cooled, cut each round in half horizontally so you have 4 layers; set aside. Mix sugar, coconut, sour cream, and whipped topping. Set 1 cup aside. Use remaining mixture to frost the layers. Add layers one on the other. Use remaining 1 cup frosting to frost outside of cake. Refrigerate 2 to 3 days.

# Grandma's Chocolate Cake

2 cups all-purpose flour

2 cups sugar

¼ cup cocoa

1 teaspoon ground cinnamon

1 cup butter or margarine

1 cup water

1 teaspoon baking soda

2 large eggs

½ cup buttermilk

1 teaspoon vanilla extract

Combine first 4 ingredients, and set aside. Combine butter and water in a large saucepan; bring to a boil. Remove from heat; stir in soda. Add flour mixture, stirring well. Stir in eggs, buttermilk, and vanilla extract. Spoon into a greased and floured 13x9x2-inch pan. Bake at 350° for 30 minutes.

## Chocolate Frosting

2 CUPS

½ cup butter or margarine

⅓ cup milk

1 (16-ounce) package powdered sugar, sifted

¼ cup cocoa

1 teaspoon vanilla extract

Combine butter and milk in a saucepan. Bring mixture to a boil; remove from heat. Combine sifted powdered sugar and cocoa; add to butter mixture. Add vanilla, stirring until smooth. Pour onto warm cake.

# Plum Pudding

### 10 TO 12 SERVINGS

3 cups all-purpose flour

1 teaspoon baking soda

¼ teaspoon salt

2 teaspoons ground cinnamon

½ teaspoon ground allspice

½ teaspoon ground cloves

2 cups raisins

1 cup peeled, chopped apple

1 cup currants

1 cup molasses

1 cup cold water

1 cup finely chopped suet

Combine flour, soda, salt, and spices in a large bowl; stir well. Stir in raisins, apple, and currants. Combine molasses, water, and suet; add to dry ingredients, stirring well. Spoon mixture into a well-greased 10-cup mold; cover tightly. Place mold on shallow rack in a large, deep kettle with enough boiling water to come halfway up mold. Cover kettle; steam pudding 3 hours in continuously boiling water (replace as needed). Unmold and serve with Hard Sauce.

# Hard Sauce

### ¾ CUP

½ cup butter or margarine, softened

1 cup sifted powdered sugar

2 to 4 tablespoons rum, sherry, or brandy

Combine butter and powdered sugar, beating until smooth. Add rum; beat until fluffy. Chill.

# Date Cake

1 teaspoon baking soda
½ pound pitted dates chopped
⅔ cup boiling water
¼ cup butter
1 ½ cups sugar
1 egg
1 teaspoon salt
2 cups flour, divided
1 teaspoon vanilla
2 ¼ cups chopped pecans

Sprinkle soda over dates. Pour boiling water over and stir well; set aside to cool.

Cream butter and sugar, add unbeaten egg; beat well. Combine salt and flour. Add one cup of flour, date mixture, another cup of flour, mix and add vanilla and pecans. Mix well.

Bake in two 8-inch cake pans or 2 small loaf pans  Bake layers at 350° for 25 minutes and loaves at 325° for 30 to 40 minutes. Place a pan of hot water in the bottom of the oven.

## Caramel Icing

3 tablespoons butter
3 cups sugar, divided
½ cup half & half
½ cup milk
Pinch salt
1 teaspoon vanilla

Place butter in a large heavy frying pan. Pour 1 cup of sugar over butter. Put 2 cups of sugar in a saucepan with half & half and milk, add salt. Bring to a boil. Caramelize sugar over medium heat. When sugar has reach a rich caramel color, pour boiling milk into sugar.

Stir rapidly and cook until 230° on a candy thermometer. cool and add vanilla. Spread on cooled cake.

# Osgood Pie

**4 egg whites**
**Yolks of 4 eggs**
**2 cups sugar**
**1 tablespoon flour**
**1 tablespoon butter**
**1 teaspoon vinegar**
**1 teaspoon cinnamon**
**1 teaspoon cloves**
**1 cup chopped pecans**
**1 cup raisins**
**2 (8-inch) pie shells**

Beat egg whites until stiff. Set aside. Beat yolks lightly. Add sugar, flour, butter, vinegar, spices, pecans, and raisins. Gently fold in egg whites.

Pour into two 8-inch unbaked pie shells. Bake 40 to 45 minutes. Cool well; pie is best if it can "age" in a cool place but not refrigerated at least one day.

# Keeping Notes

*Recipes To Remember*

# Keeping Notes

*Recipes To Remember*

# Index

# Homemade Christmas

Wimmer Cookbook Distribution
4210 B. F. Goodrich Boulevard
Memphis, Tennessee 38118

Please send _____ copies of *Homemade Christmas*
@ $15.95 each _____
Tennessee residents add sales tax @ $1.32 each _____
Postage and handling @ $5.00 each _____
Total _____

Charge to Visa (    ) or MasterCard (    )

# _____ Expiration Date _____

Signature _____

Name_____

Address _____

City_____ State _____ Zip _____

## Cookbook Lovers Take Note...

If you've enjoyed **Homemade Christmas**, The Wimmer
Companies, Inc., has a catalog of 250 other cookbook titles
that may interest you. To receive your free copy, write:

The Wimmer Companies, Inc.
4210 B. F. Goodrich Boulevard
Memphis, Tennessee 38118

or call 1-800-727-1034